Packhorses in Wales and the Artist

The reproduction shown on the first page is of a drawing, previously unpublished, by Simon De Koster. The original is in The National Library of Wales, Aberystwyth.

Simon De Koster was born in Middelburg, the Netherlands, in 1767. He studied at the Academy there and in 1788 he came to London where he died in 1831.

How could a young painter establish himself in London? He set up as a portraitist. If he could persuade famous people to sit for him – people with cash to spend on a portrait – he could earn his keep while gaining reputation by association with the great and the good.

He chose his subject with care, capturing, among others, two of the most celebrated personalities of the age: Admiral Horatio Nelson (1758–1805) of Trafalgar fame; William Pitt (1759–1806), prime minister of Great Britain (1783–1801, 1804–6). The latter portrait has been judged a brilliant impression.

That the artist was not devoted to the upper crust is indicated in his choice of other subjects. There is his depiction of a rabbit catcher, spade on one shoulder, staff holding his catch on the other. And there are his drawings of everyday scenes including his packhorse subject.

Did the Dutch painter come to Wales for refreshment from the London scene? Was he imprisoned by necessity in the city, always seeking escape to the natural nuances nearest his heart, the inspirations which could only be discovered in the countryside?

Through his art we can gaze and gaze upon what packhorses, packhorse trails and packhorsemen were like in Wales in the late eighteenth and early nineteenth centuries.

Ralph Maddern

Walk **Snowdonia**

ancient trackways
Roman roads
packhorse trails

By the same author

	ISBN
Walk in the beautiful Conwy Valley	1–872050–00
Walk in magnificent Snowdonia	1–872050–02–6
Walk Snowdonia Peaks	0–9505053–9–0
Walk in the Vale of Ffestiniog	0–9505053–6–6

to Sam Joe Robert

Focus Publications Ltd

© Ralph Maddern

First published in Great Britain 1981
Revised and re-published 1992

Focus Publications Ltd
9 Priors Road
Windsor
Berkshire SL4 4PD

ISBN: 1–872050–03–4

Printed in Great Britain by
Grosvenor Press (Portsmouth) Ltd.

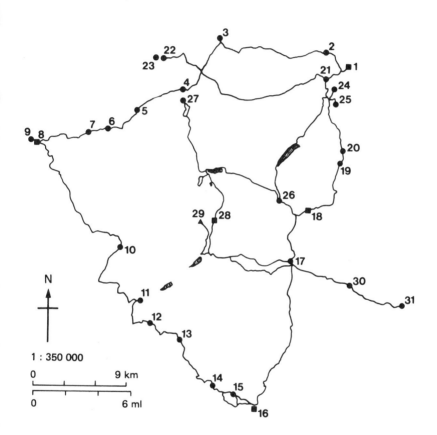

Walk	ancient	Roman	packhorse
Snowdonia	trackways	roads	trails

1. CANOVIUM
2. Ro-wen
3. Aber
4. Rachub
5. Rhiwlas
6. Penisa'r Waun
7. Llanrug
8. SEGONTIUM
9. Caernarfon
10. Rhyd-ddu

11. Beddgelert
12. Nantmor
13. Croesor
14. Maentwrog
15. Gellilydan
16. TOMEN-Y-MUR
17. Dolwyddelan
18. CAER LLUGWY
19. Llanrhychwyn
20. Trefriw
21. Llanbedr-y-cennin

22. Tal-y-bont
23. Llandegai
24. Tal-y-bont
25. Dolgarrog
26. Capel Curig
27. Bethesda
28. Pen-y-gwryd
29. Pen-y-Pass
30. Penmachno
31. Ysbyty Ifan

Illustrations

by

Outline Portraits

Contents

Compass Bearings

Pedometer Readings

and Snowdonia

Accuracy of position and direction is ensured by combining two kinds of measurement: distance registered by a pedometer, and direction recorded by a compass.

A pedometer reading may be taken to be correct to the nearest one-tenth of a kilometre or one hundred metres: 1.7km is within the range 1.65km to 1.75km, 1650 metres to 1750 metres,

A compass bearing of 080° can be accepted as lying within the arc 075° to 085°.

To determine a bearing, hold a hand compass in a horizontal position and allow the needle to steady. Turn the circle graduated in degrees until the N/S marking – 0°/360° to 180° – lies exactly beneath the needle.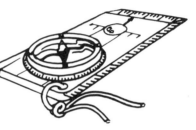

If a bearing in this text is to be followed move the base platform until its centre line registers the required reading on the graduated circle.

If the bearing of an object from a position on the ground is required, move the base platform until its centreline is aligned with the object. Read the object's bearing on the graduated circle.

If seeking a bearing from an Ordnance Survey map in order to follow a direction on the ground,

★ place the centre of the graduated circle on the map position from which the bearing is to be taken

★ move the grid lines of the graduated circle to coincide with those of the OS map

★ Align the base platform's centreline on the map with the object whose bearing is required and read the bearing on the graduated circle.

Welsh

Place names in Wales are fascinating because of the descriptions they offer of their locations. That is why interpretations are given where this is possible. Understanding what the name means is often a major clue to knowing the place itself. Pronunciation can be quite difficult for a non-Welsh speaker but it is worth trying to get the right sound. The main sounds, where these differ from English, are set out below.

a	as in *are*
c	always hard as in *car*
Ch	as in the Scottish *loch*
e	"ay" as in *say*
f	as in the English *"v"*
Ff	as in the English *"f"*
g	always hard as in *give*
Ll	place the tongue to form "l" but emit a passage of air through the tongue to merge with the following letter
r	rolled more strongly than in English
Rh	both the "r" and the "h" are pronounced
Th	as in *both*
Dd	also "th" but as in *this*
u	"i" as in *it* or "ee" as in *feet*
w	"oo" as in roost (Llanrwst = Llanroost) – it also works like the English "w"
y	"u" as in *fun* or "ee" as in *feet* or "i" as in *pin* (you have to listen)

J, K, Q, V, X and Z do not appear in Welsh as these sounds are conveyed by other letters or diphthongs.

As with some Welsh poetry the evocative quality in the term *critch-cratch* eludes adequate representation in English. *Critch-cratch* refers to a gate hung in a U or V-shaped enclosure and is, therefore, impassable to stock animals. It is sometimes known as a "kissing gate".

Critch-cratch seems much more illustrative and evocative.

Countryside
COMMISSION

YOUR RIGHTS OF WAY ARE
Public footpaths – on foot only. *Sometimes waymarked in yellow*
Bridleways – on foot, horseback and pedal cycle. *Sometimes waymarked in blue*
Byways (usually old roads), most "Roads Used as Public Paths" and, of course, public roads – all traffic.
Use maps, signs and waymarks. Ordnance Survey Pathfinder and Landranger maps show most public rights of way.

ON RIGHTS OF WAY YOU CAN
Take a pram, pushchair or wheelchair if practicable
Take a dog (on a lead or under close control)
Take a short route round an illegal obstruction or remove it sufficiently to get past.

YOU HAVE A RIGHT TO GO FOR RECREATION TO
Public parks and open spaces – on foot
Most commons near older towns and cities – on foot and sometimes on horseback
Private land where the owner has a formal agreement with the local authority.

IN ADDITION you can *use* by local or established *custom or consent*, but ask for advice if you're unsure:
Many areas of open country like moorland, fell and coastal areas, especially those of the National Trust, and some commons
Some woods and forests, especially those owned by the Forestry Commission
Country Parks and picnic sites
Most beaches
Canal towpaths
Some private paths and tracks.
Consent sometimes extends to riding horses and pedal cycles.

FOR YOUR INFORMATION
County councils and London boroughs maintain and record rights of way, and register commons
Obstructions, dangerous animals, harassment and misleading signs on rights of way are illegal and you should report them to the county council
Paths across fields can be ploughed, but must normally be reinstated within two weeks
Landowners can require you to leave land to which you have no right of access
Motor vehicles are normally permitted only on roads, byways and some "Roads Used as Public Paths"
Follow any local bylaws.

AND, WHEREVER YOU GO, FOLLOW THE COUNTRY CODE
Enjoy the countryside and respect its life and work
Guard against all risk of fire
Fasten all gates
Keep your dogs under close control
Keep to public paths across farmland
Use gates and stiles to cross fences, hedges and walls
Leave livestock, crops and machinery alone
Take your litter home
Help to keep all water clean
Protect wildlife, plants and trees
Take special care on country roads
Make no unnecessary noise.

This Charter is for practical guidance in England and Wales only. Fuller advice is given in a free booklet "Out in the country" available from Countryside Commission Publications Despatch Department, 19–23 Albert Road, Manchester M19 2EQ.

Published with grant aid from the **Countryside** COMMISSION

CEFn Gwlad

DYMA EICH HAWLIAU TRAMWY

Llwybrau cyhoeddus – ar droed yn unig. *Fe'u dynodir weithiau â'r lliw melyn*

Llwybrau ceffyl – ar droed, ar gefn ceffyl neu feic. *Fe'u dynodir weithiau â'r lliw glas*

Cilffyrdd (hen ffyrdd fel arfer), y mwyafrif o "Ffyrdd a Ddefnyddir fel Llwybrau Cyhoeddus" ac wrth gwrs, ffyrdd cyhoeddus – pob trafnidiaeth. Defnyddiwch fapiau, arwyddion a mynegbyst. *Dangosir y mwyafrif o hawliau tramwy cyhoeddus ar fapiau Pathfinder a Landranger yr Arolwg Ordnans.*

LLE BO HAWLIAU TRAMWY GALLWCH

Fynd â phram, coets gadair neu gadair olwyn os yw'n ymarferol

Fynd â chi (ar dennyn neu dan reolaeth glos)

Gymryd ffordd fer o gwmpas rhwystr anghyfreithlon neu ei symud ddigon i fynd heibio iddo.

MAE GENNYCH HAWL I FYND I HAMDDENA

Mewn parciau cyhoeddus a mannau agored – ar droed

I'r mwyafrif o diroedd comin gerllaw hen drefi a dinasoedd – ar droed ac weithiau ar gefn ceffyl

Ar dir preifat lle mae gan y perchennog gytundeb ffurfiol â'r awdurdod lleol.

YN OGYSTAL gallwch *ddefnyddio* trwy arfer neu ganiatâd *lleol neu sefydlog* ond gofynnwch am gyngor os ydych yn ansicr:

Llawer darn o dir agored fel rhostir, bryniau a'r arfordir, yn enwedig rhai'r Ymddiriedolaeth Genedlaethol a rhai tiroedd comin.

Rhai coedlannau a choedwigoedd, yn enwedig y rhai sy'n eiddo i'r Comisiwn Coedwigaeth

Parciau Gwledig a safleoedd picnic

Mwyafrif ein traethau

Llwybrau ymyl y camlesi

Rhai llwybrau a thraciau preifat

Estynnir caniatâd weithiau i gynnwys mynd ar gefn ceffyl neu feic.

ER GWYBODAETH I CHI

Mae cynghorau sir a bwrdeisdrefi Llundain yn cynnal a chofnodi hawliau tramwy, ac yn cofrestru tir comin

Mae rhwystrau, anifeiliaid peryglus, erledigaeth ac arwyddion camarweiniol yn anghyfreithlon a dylech roi gwybod i'r cyngor sir amdanynt

Gellir aredig llwybrau sy'n croesi caeau, ond rhaid eu hadfer o fewn pythefnos fel arfer

Gall tirfeddiannwyr fynnu eich bod yn gadael tir lle nad oes gennych hawl mynediad

Ni chaniateir moduron fel arfer ond ar ffyrdd, cilffyrdd a rhai "Ffyrdd a Ddefnyddir fel Llwybrau Cyhoeddus"

Parchwch unrhyw is-ddeddfau lleol

A, LLE BYNNAG YR EWCH, DILYNWCH Y RHEOLAU CEFN GWLAD

Mwynhewch y wlad a pharchwch ei bywyd a'i gwaith

Gwyliwch rhag holl beryglon tân

Caewch bob llidiard

Cadwch eich cŵn dan reolaeth glos

Cadwch at lwybrau cyhoeddus wrth groesi tir amaethyddol

Defnyddiwch lidiardau a chamfeydd i groesi ffensys, gwrychoedd a waliau

Gadewch lonydd i anifeiliaid, cnydau a pheiriannau

Ewch â'ch sbwriel adre gyda chi

Helpwch gadw pob dŵr yn lân

Cymerwch ofal o goed, creaduriaid a phlanhigion gwyllt

Byddwch yn ofalus iawn ar ffyrdd gwledig

Peidiwch â chreu sŵn yn ddiangen

Arweiniad ymarferol yw'r canllawiau hyn yng Nghymru a Lloegr yn unig. Ceir cyngor manylach o Swyddfa Cymru, Comisiwn Cefn Gwlad, Tŷ Ladywell, Y Drenewydd, Powys SŶ16 1RD.

Cyhoeddwyd gyda chymorth ariannol  **COMISIWN Cefn Gwlad**

Eryri pathmakers

Aeons of time in pathmaking

The beginning goes back almost to the end of the Ice Age, about 10,000 years ago. As the glaciers retreated from the British Isles, animals migrated across the landscape, and humans who were hunters and gatherers, followed the animal tracks. Snowdonia would have retained its ice cap longer than the lowland areas, but its altitudes and ruggedness have ensured that much of what was impressed upon these mountains has remained. Many of the pre-historic routes have survived cultivation, allowing us to enjoy a heritage extending back about 7,000 years – long before the Romans arrived. Fortunately, some of the tracks are marked by standing stones and cromlechs which ancient peoples erected. Probably the best examples are to be found along the trackway through *Bwlch y Ddeufaen* – the pass of the two stones – referring to the two standing stones 3 miles west of Ro-wen, the first on the left of the track, the second 80 metres ahead on the right. These stones served to mark the track near the top of the pass through what would have been, in pre-historic times, a remote and dangerous area.

Nearer the coast the stone circle, Maeni Hirion, above Penmaenmawr, indicates a trackway intersection for routes east, west, north and south. Excavations have shown that Stone Age, Bronze Age and Iron Age peoples used these trackways. As well as the main tracks there were others connecting groups of round huts. We see from the hut remains that these settlements were clustered on defensible sites where there was an assured water supply and grazing for animals.

The Romans used the old trackway routes where these suited their purposes. However, in order to accommodate wheeled vehicles as well as marching columns, they needed constructed roads. These were of two kinds: the main military roads connecting forts, and secondary routes between camps and settlements.

There were four principal Roman forts in the Snowdonia area: Canovium (Caerhun), Segontium (Caernarfon), Tomen-y-mur (near Llan Ffestiniog) and Caer Llugwy (Bryn-y-gefeilia, near Betws-y-coed). Construction was completed by the beginning of the second century AD. The exact sites and designs of the forts are known but very little has been proven about the roads. Only a few short stretches at higher levels have been positively identified. Therefore, most of the actual routes remain a matter of conjecture.

There is less uncertainty about packhorse trails. After the Romans departed from Snowdonia about 390AD, wheeled transport suffered a lapse of use for about fourteen centuries. During that long period, Snowdonians relied upon pack-animals to move about their mountainous domain. The trails they evolved blended perfectly with the topography. Of course, like their predecessors, they used earlier routes, including Roman roads. Therefore, the walks described here use a synthesis of routes developed over three historical periods of time: the trackways of the ancient Britons, the arterial roads of Imperial Rome and the packhorse trails of the pre-industrial age.

Canovium (Caerhun)

When the Romans decided to conquer Wales and northern England, about 70 AD, they saw Deva (Chester) as the ideal site for a base fort. Both campaigns could be served from Deva and supplies could be shipped in by sea.

Canovium was established about 78 AD. Situated near the upper tidal limit of the River Conwy, its role was to guard the junction of roads that led west and south. The remains of the fort may be observed as an embanked square rising about five feet above field level. It covered an area of about five acres. Extensive excavations were carried out from 1926 to 1929. The only part of the site not investigated lies beneath Caerhun Church which occupies the NE quarter of the fort area. It is thought that the garrison would have numbered about 500 infantry and cavalry. Occupation continued at

Canovium until about the middle of the second century when it became a civilian settlement. To the east, between the fort and the River Conwy, are the remains of Roman baths.

Caerhun derives from Rhûn, a prince of Gwynedd who lived here in the sixth century. The Parish Church of St Mary dates from the fourteenth century; its chancel is of the fifteenth century, the south chapel sixteenth century and the lich-gate eighteenth century.

Canovium – Segontium: 41.3km, 25.8ml

Canovium – Aber: 15.7km, 9.8ml.

From St Mary's Church, Caerhun (00km), bear W to the B5106 (0.5km) and turn right (N); 250m along the road veer left and continue for 500m to a stile (1.0km). Turn right (N), cross the field to a council road (1.2km) and continue past Llican-isaf and Llican-uchaf (1.4km) to the Ty'n-y-groes – Ro-wen road (2.2km). We are now on or near the ancient Roman route from Deva (Chester) to Segontium. Turn left (W) and follow the road to Ro-wen (3.2km, 2ml).

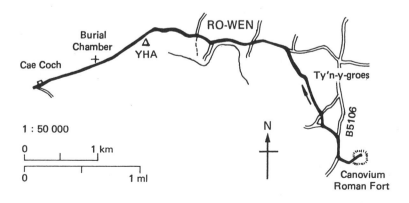

Ro-wen

A camp by the white Ro, flowing pure and crystalline from the mountains, the Carneddau. Plenty of fish and game to store up before the climb, or to replenish after the long trail through the pass from the west coast and Anglesey. Pleasant green fields with good grazing.

The main staging post west of the Conwy River at the foot of the Carneddau on the road between Canovium and Segontium. The local tribe, the Ordovices, fought fiercely to defend their settlement and could only be defeated by a concentration of superior power. Afterwards they provided useful labour for road building.

Because Roman power remained under challenge, a fort had to be built on Pen-y-gaer, that high dome to the south, from where the whole of the lower Conwy could be kept under surveillance. The raiders from across the Irish Sea were especially troublesome. They would appear in their black coracles and sweep up river on a high tide, pillaging and destroying. But signals from Pen-y-gaer could give warning of the approaching threat.

After the Romans had departed, the scene settled into the way it had been centuries earlier. Nothing changed very much for more than a millenium. The pack pony came into its own as the ever reliable, infinitely flexible transport mode, wonderfully attuned to these mountains, knowing its own way along the trails.

Continue from the Ro-wen PO up the road for 200m, fork-right and climb the steep hill to the Youth Hostel (4.3km).

Tranquillity settles as one glances back to the Conwy Valley and the meandering river flowing slowly from the heartland of Snowdonia. The first example of Roman road becomes evident about 100m before reaching the burial chamber. It appears as a raised shelf on the hillside adjacent to the existing track (map ref: 742718; elevation 330m, 1000ft) and bears 250°. The megalithic burial chamber, (5.0km, 3.1ml) is

cromlech builders

a reminder that this is one of the oldest tracks in Britain.

A place to rest on the ancient route and to contemplate how that massive capstone was lodged so neatly upon the four upright stones countless years before the Romans trod this way.

About 650m further on there is another pre-Roman construction in the form of an upright stone, 2.5m high (map ref: 736717).

Following the Roman road and ancient trackway we join a council road (6.0km) which rises from Llanbedr-y~cennin. The modern road and the ancient one straddle each other, veering to NW between the two standing stones which gave this Pass its name: Bwlch y Ddeufaen. The first standing stone on the left (7.8km, 4.9ml) is 3m high; 80m ahead on the right (330°) is the second, which is 2m high. *Bwlch* means gap, *deu* or *ddeu* two, *maen* or *faen* stone. *Bwlch y Ddeufaen:* gap of the two stones.

The track winds on through the bald Pass. To the north is the mountain, Penmaemawr, where there was once an ancient fort, Braich y Ddinas. Here the Ordovices were well dug in to challenge the invaders. A bypass by the mobile conquerors round the south of the mountain could enclose the defenders against the northern sea making capture inevitable.

Now the ancient fort has been carried away as loads of quarried stone. Penmaenmawr has been a quarry for 5000 years from the time when it provided raw material for *graiglwyd* stone axes which were widely distributed in Wales

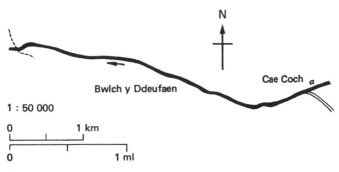

N

Bwlch y Ddeufaen

Cae Coch

1 : 50 000

0   1 km

0   1 ml

18

trade in stone

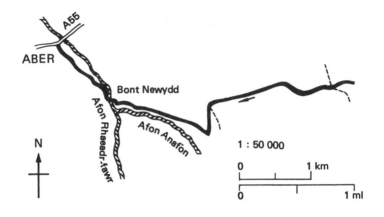

and England as articles of trade. The stone's hard and durable consistency, and good flaking property, made it a highly valued resource at a time when Britain's New Stone Age cultivators were clearing forests.

The Roman road veered NW in the direction of Llanfairfechan which can be glimpsed far below. Perhaps a branch road descended to the coast; but the main route must have turned towards Segontium, roughly on a bearing of 240°. However, every trace of it has vanished, although there have been discoveries indicating its probable route.

Follow the track westward and then S to a gate (12.8km, 8.0ml) which marks the boundary of National Trust guardianship. We are now using a packhorse trail which began at the ferry opposite Tal-y-cafn; we followed the ancient routes through the Pass and continued down to *Bont Newydd* – new bridge (14.5km, 9.1ml) – which spans the *Afon Rhaeadr-fawr* – river of the big falls. The river tumbles over Aber Falls about a mile upstream. The bridge is called *new* because in the early nineteenth century it replaced the ford which packhorse drivers used for countless years. Stones placed to assist packhorsemen crossing the river may be observed beneath the bridge.

Along the road is Aber village (15.7km, 9.8ml).

packhorse ford

The main packhorse trail across the Carneddau in the eighteenth century is shown opposite.

The reproduction represents part of a work by John Evans who published a map of six counties of North Wales in 1795. The map shows the trail rising from the west bank of the Conwy River, opposite Tal-y-cafn, to Tynygroes, up to the route of the Roman road through Bwylch y Ddeufaen, on to the Bont Newydd ford of the Afon Rhaeadr-fawr and along to Aber village.

In Bwlch y Ddeufaen there was a fork where the trail from Llanbedr-y-cennin, Talybont, Trefriw, and other settlements further south, joined the trail through Ty'n-y-groes.

From Aber the trail continued along the shortest route to Anglesey – across Lafan Sands. But on reaching the Menai Strait the crossing had to be completed by ferry. In order to aid travellers on this hazardous journey of about four miles, subject as it was to incoming tides, inclement weather and uncertainties of the ferry, a bell was continuously rung in Aber whenever sea fog descended.

An even longer route across Lafan Sands originated in Penmaen village, as Penmaenmawr was then.

Aber

Aber is a parish rich in historical remains. A short distance from the post office – second turning left along the falls road and round to the right – is an eleventh-century Norman earthwork, known as Pen y Mwd. In the thirteenth century there was a residence of the princes of Gwynedd in Aber, and it is thought that this may have been its site.

Across the Afon Aber from the village is the house, Pen-y-bryn, dating from the sixteenth century, and, 500m to the SE, enclosed in woodland, is the site of a hillfort, *Maes y Gaer* – field of the fort – whose date is uncertain.

The Parish Church of St Bedfan, which stands apart from the village, 300m to the W, was rebuilt in 1878. A much older church stood on the site now taken up by the cemetery.

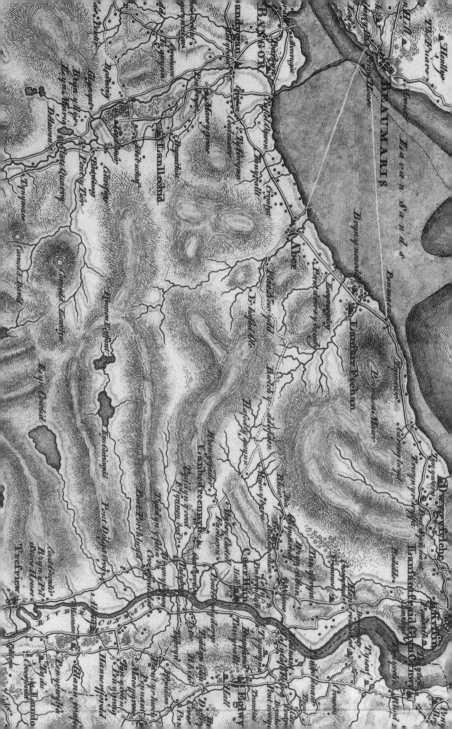

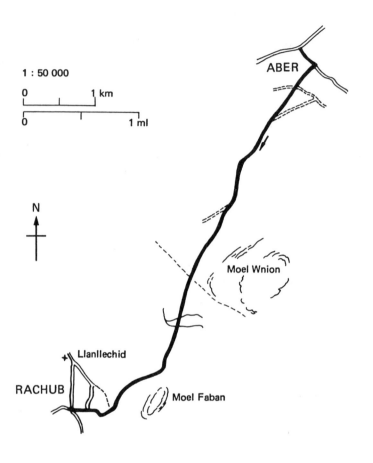

1 : 50 000

0   1 km

0   1 ml

N

ABER

Moel Wnion

Llanllechid

RACHUB

Moel Faban

    The remains of stone huts show that the valley was fairly closely settled in pre-historic times. The main settlement was about 500m downstream from the falls where a community lived in rectangular and round huts. These settlers cultivated small levelled fields and grazed animals which they would have had to protect from wolves. In the cwm above the falls there are further remains of pre-Roman settlement.

    Nearby are trackways and packhorse trails along which we can walk south-west towards Segontium.

Aber – Rachub – Rhiwlas: 12.3km, 7.7ml.

From Aber PO (00km) walk SE along the falls road to
the second path (0.4km), turn right and after 30m fork left
(250°) up the hill to a stile (0.6km). Here is a point from
which to view the sweep of coastline from Penmaenmawr
along to the Strait, and the Anglesey coast where the town of
Beaumaris (320°) marks the terminus of the old packhorse
trail across the Lafan Sands. A function of the castle at
Beaumaris was to guard this tidal route.

Cross the farm track, 100m further up, continue SW
through a belt of plantation to a stile (0.9km) and on to a
packhorse trail (1.2km) which bears 240°. The view widens
as one follows the trail to a bridged culvert (2.6km) where a
path veers left (210°) to a stile (2.9km). The path crosses the
knees of the bald mound, Moel Wnion (580m, 1900ft) and,
descending, there is a view on the right of Llanllechid
Church, standing beyond an extensive area of early habitation
sites. These include remains of round huts, long huts,
enclosed and unenclosed hut-groups (map refs: 629688;
632687; 632685; 631684).

Skirt round Moel Faban (408m, 1340ft) on the left and
prepare for a different historical period.

As if entering a medieval town, one arrives at a gate
(6.2km), 100m beyond which is a left turn into Rachub High
Street. Descend across rows of terraced cottages, once occupied by quarrymen and their families, to Llanllechid PO
(6.7km, 4.2ml), a name which illustrates that this village has
two names: Rachub and Llanllechid.

Rachub

Stand at the bottom of High Street and imagine quarrymen descending from the rows of terraces in early morning.
Tramp, tramp, tramp went the hobnail boots through the
square, away to grey rock faces and dark caverns.

Chapel three times on Sunday; again on Tuesday evening for a prayer meeting; and on Friday for hymn practice. It was a way of life now remembered with affection.

Those were times when people were part of a community that could share and enjoy simple pleasures at low cost. On a public holiday, families would gather in the square and walk in a group to the beach beyond Aber Ogwen. When the tide was out, some would walk across the sand to the channel opposite Beaumaris to gather the large cockles that grew in the mud there. Driftwood was collected and fires lit for boiling water which was drawn from a special well back from the beach. After making tea the families would settle for a picnic. At the end of the afternoon they walked the four miles back to the village, singing as they went along.

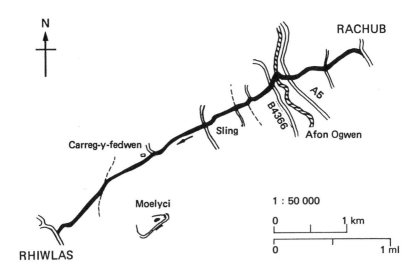

Continue westward across the A5 (8.0km), the Afon Ogwen (8.2km) and the B4366 (8.4km) to a lane which rises to a council road (8.6km). Turn left (SW) and follow the road for 400m to a gate where a path bears 260°. At 9.4km turn left, then right (W) past a chapel on the left to a council road and the hamlet of Sling (9.6km).

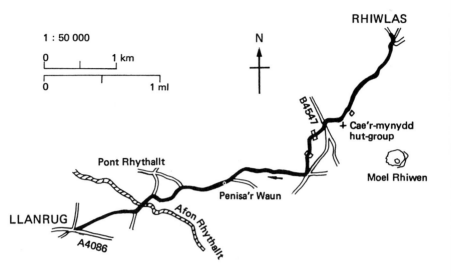

Across the road to the left is a lane, bearing 250°, leading to *Carreg-y-fedwen* – stone of the birch. About 50m before reaching the farmhouse turn left (10.6km) onto a delightfully green path of deep forest solitude. Continue to a wall gate (11.0km), along the boundary wall round the base of Moelyci to critch-cratch 1 (11.4km), across a lane and SW to critch-cratch 2 (11.8km). Follow the path past a terrace of cottages to critch-cratch 3 (12.0km), turn right to critch-cratch 4 and left down to Rhiwlas PO (12.3km, 7.7ml).

Rhiwlas

Why did the Celts select this area for close settlement? Well, there were the two hills, Moel Rhiwen (392m, 1283ft) to the south and Moelyci (397m, 1301ft) to the east. About a mile and a half to the west was the hill, Pen Dinas (168m, 556ft). These three heights overlooked arable land suitable for cultivation.

For a period of about 800 years, from the late Bronze

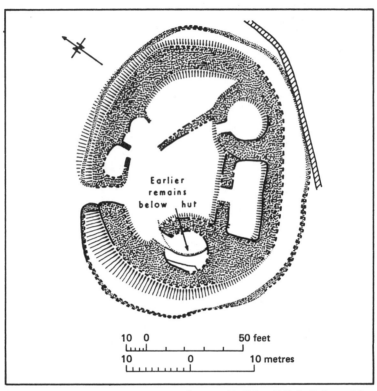

Earlier
remains
below   hut

10 0   50 feet

10   0   10 metres

From An *Inventory of the Ancient Monuments in Caernarvonshire Volume II*. Used with the permission of the Controller of Her Majesty's Stationery Office.

Age to the end of the Roman occupation, hillforts and enclosed hut-groups were a typical form of settlement. Effective defence was a fundamental condition of living. Hilltops provided ideal sites. Thick defensive walls could be erected from the plentiful supply of stone available in this area.

Such measures did not effectively hinder the Romans who established their power in north Wales after a thorough slaughter of local inhabitants. However, in the later Roman period the re-occupation of hillforts was tolerated by the conquerors. Faced with increasing harassment by raiders from across the Irish Sea and northern Britain in the third and

fourth centuries, Romans and native inhabitants found a measure of mutual interest in meeting outside threats.

A short distance along this route from Rhiwlas there is an interesting site where a pre-historic extended family once lived.

Rhiwlas – Penisa'r Waun – Llanrug – Segontium: 13.3km, 8.3ml.

From the PO (00km) bear SE uphill for 100m, turn right (210°) opposite St George's Church and follow the lane to critch-cratches 1 (0.3km), 2 (0.4km), 3 (1.0km) and Cae'r-mynydd farmhouse (1.4km). About 150m beyond the farmhouse (map ref: 572647) are the remains of an oval enclosure, 110ft by 85ft.

It was entered through a passageway from the NW. There was an outer wall of large boulders and then an inner wall 12ft thick. Standing in the courtyard facing N, there was, from the entrance moving clockwise: a rectangular room 16ft by 10ft; a round hut about 9ft in diameter; a wall projecting into the courtyard for about 32ft behind which other undetermined structures probably existed; a round hut 21ft in diameter; a rectangular hut 39ft by 16ft; against the SW wall of the enclosure, a round hut 22ft in diameter. When the site was excavated in 1949 and 1955 it was discovered that there had been more than one period of occupation. Pottery dating from the third and fourth centuries was found; there was evidence of a clay hearth, a paved floor, a stone bench and a small storage pit.

These people were crop farmers as well as pastoralists – they cultivated terraced fields. When attackers came the defenders would not have fought alone. Up the slopes of *Moel Rhiwen* – white hill – and even on its summit, there were hut-groups where neighbours could be called upon for assistance.

Standing in the courtyard one tries to imagine what it was like to live here, and what happened when the Roman army arrived.

Follow the path to critch-cratch 4 (1.8km), cross the

B4547 to critch-cratch 5 and continue to the house Fron Chwith (2.1km). Fork left to critch-cratch 6 (2.0km) and the farmhouse *Blaen Cae-isaf* – which means end of the lower field (2.2km). Follow the farm drive to a council road (2.7km) and turn right (NW) to the village of Penisa'r Waun (3.7km, 2.3ml).

Penisa'r Waun

One of the few Roman milestones recovered in Snowdonia was found a little more than a half-mile SE of the village (map ref: 567636). It is now in the Segontium Museum. Less than a half-mile in the opposite direction are the remains of pre-historic hut-groups (map refs: 550637; 549641).

Pen means end or top; *isaf* lower; *waun* or *waen* higher pasture. *Penisa'r Waun:* lower end of the higher pasture.

Continue westward for 800m to a lane on the left (SW), fork right (NW) at 5.0km to a council road and turn left (W) to Pont Rhythallt (5.4km). Fork right after crossing the bridge and continue to Llanrug (6.4km, 4.0ml).

Llanrug

This village gives one the impression of a plant that has sprouted haphazardly along branches of road. On an outer twig is the Parish Church of St Michael, dating from the thirteenth century and attended by a notable cemetery. In most communities the church occupies a central position but here it is isolated from the main part of the village. Why was it put where it is? The answer seems to be the nineteenth-century routing of the main road, the present A4086. This determined the location of almost all subsequent development – at least half a mile from what was once the medieval village where the church had presided in its accustomed place.

During the time of transformation, when Llanrug was developing in this unusual way, there lived here a colourful character whose life illustrated a most engaging aspect of Welsh rural life. Foulk Roberts was a quarryman who liked to go up into the heather to play his flute. He took a notebook with him and it was said that his "lovely notes spread over the district mingled with the smell of heather." He taught music in schools and churches. He played in inns and country houses. Llanrug's first brass band developed under his instruction. Foulk was a prodigious walker, always travelling on foot, and he was an enthusiastic writer and collector of songs. As well as his own songs he wrote down those composed by others so they would not be lost and forgotten. In the National Library there are 650 compositions in his collection; 150 of them are his own work.

In 1835 a school was built in Llanrug. As part of a celebration, the village children marched from the church, where classes had been held up to that time, to the new school which was called *Ysgoldy Glanmoelyn*. Foulk Roberts marched at their head, playing his flute and leading the children in song. It was a joyous time for Llanrug.

Foulk's way of life did not bring him riches; he died poor and lies buried in Llanrug churchyard under a grave-

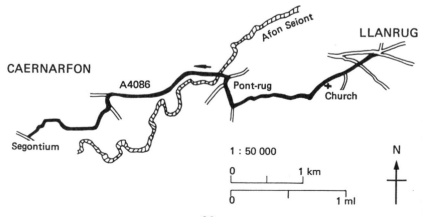

flutist and audience

stone erected by friends. But his songs are remembered and his personality can charm even after more than a century.

Cross the A4086 (6.4km) and fork right (7.0km) along a lane to the Parish Church (7.4km). Follow the lane to a council road (9.2km), turn right (N), right again (9.6km) to the A4086 and left over Pont-rug.

At 11.5km turn left, left again 100m further on and right (11.7km) onto a grass lane. Continue SW to critch-cratch 7 (12.0km), SW and W to critch-cratch 8 (12.3km) and, 100m further on, fork right (NW) to a housing estate. Take the second turning left (W), left into Cae'r Saint, left then right into Hyfrydle, and on to the Segontium Museum alongside the A4085 (13.3km, 8.3ml).

Segontium/Caernarfon

From the steps of the museum one can look over the town to the Menai Strait and Anglesey beyond. This hill (elevation: 46m, 150ft) was a Roman headquarters for more than 300 years. The choice of site must have been obvious. Anglesey was a significant source of metals, especially copper; passage across and through the Strait had to be made secure.

The British chieftain, Caractacus, who had led armed resistance to the Romans when they invaded Britain in 43 AD, fled to north Wales after a series of defeats and joined the Ordovices. Here, Caractacus was defeated yet again. He escaped to join the Brigantes in northern Britain, intending no doubt, to carry on the struggle there. But he was betrayed and handed over to the conquerors who took him to Rome where they kept him a prisoner for the rest of his days.

The building of Segontium began about the year 78. Timber and earthwork structures sufficed for the first two or three decades. Then permanent buildings began to be erected in local stone and Cheshire sandstone. There was a commandant's house, a headquarters-building, workshops, barracks and two granaries. A wall was built round the fort's area of

5.7 acres. It was rectangular in shape, 550ft by 450ft, and had rounded corners. There was a gate in each of the four sides. The site of the SE gate lies beneath the Beddgelert road which cuts through the southern half of the fort. Surrounding the wall were two defensive ditches, each possibly containing a row of sharpened stakes. Fully garrisoned, Segontium was a base for about 1000 men. Occupation continued until the year 383.

In the following centuries the old fort fell into ruin. Eventually, it disappeared beneath the landscape and beyond human memory. Other conquerors came. Nine hundred years after the last Roman soldier departed from Segontium, English soldiers of King Edward the First's army arrived. At once, they began building the castle and town walls.

The Welsh were affronted. Caernarfon was a place of residence for Welsh princes and their court. In 1294, the year after the English conquest, the Welsh seized the town and held it for several months. When the revolt was put down building work was resumed at a rapid pace. By 1287 the castle and town walls were substantially complete and for the next four centuries Caernarfon was a strategic fortress.

In 1401, when Wales had risen in rebellion, the castle came under siege by insurgents displaying the standard of the rebel leader, Owain Glyndwr – a golden dragon on a white background. In 1403–4, the besiegers were joined by French forces.

As a bastion of the Royalist cause in the Civil Wars of 1642-51, the castle was besieged and taken three times. At the Restoration in 1660, Charles II ordered that the castle and town walls be demolished. Fortunately, the divine right of kings had been abolished by the victory of Parliament; the royal order was ignored and Caernarfon's great monuments survived to become a world-famous feature of Wales.

The medieval town can still be observed behind its 6ft-thick walls, 28ft high with towers rising to 40ft. There are four gates. Water Gate, nearest the castle, and Porth-yr-aur – golden gate – face the Afon Seiont (or Saint). On the eastern side is Green Gate, opening towards Castle Square, and East

Gate, providing the main access to the town. The latter is also known as Exchequer Gate because above it was housed the Exchequer for north Wales.

In the far northern corner of the medieval town is the Church of St Mary, dating from the thirteenth century and traditionally known as the Garrison Chapel. A most fascinating feature is that the Church has its vestry within a wall tower from which one may look out over the Strait.

After the medieval period the town began to grow beyond the walls. By the nineteenth century it was creeping up the hill. In sinking foundations much older footings were discovered. From about 1845, remains of the old fort were exposed. In the near vicinity other structures dating from the Roman period were revealed. There was *Hen Waliau* – Old Walls – a rectangular compound 230ft by 165ft. Its walls are 6ft thick rising to a height of 16ft. It is about 200 yards west of the fort.

Caernarfon was uncovering its ancient history.

Excavation and assessment continue. Much yet remains to be discovered about Segontium and Caernarfon.

Between the two ancient forts, Segontium in Caernarfon and Tomen-y-mur near Llan Ffestiniog, there was once a Roman road all of which is now obliterated. Yet the topography has resisted encroachment sufficiently to allow its ambience to be savoured: along paths, tracks, trails that are eternally *Eryri*, in its remoteness, ruggedness, timelessness.

Segontium – Tomen-y-mur: 45.8km, 28.6ml

Segontium – Rhyd-ddu: 16.0km,10ml

From the gate of the museum (00km) walk SE in the track of the Roman road, now the A4085, to the Parish Church of St Peblig (0.2km). Here is a church with distinctive

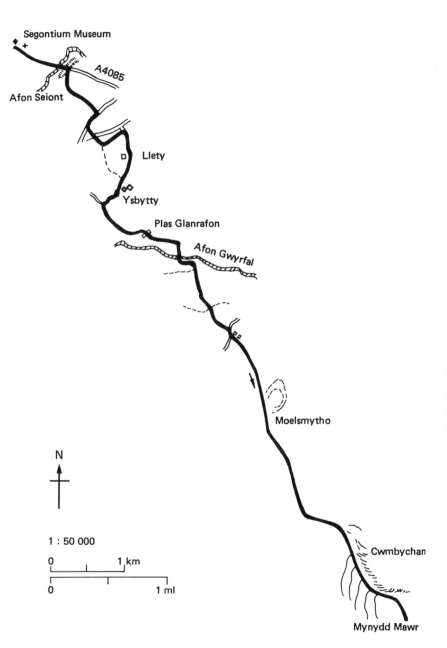

Segontium Museum

A4085

Afon Seiont

Llety

Ysbytty

Plas Glanrafon

Afon Gwyrfal

Moelsmytho

N

1 : 50 000

0   1 km

0   1 ml

Cwmbychan

Mynydd Mawr

windows and stonework. It dates from the fourteenth century but probably succeeded an earlier Celtic church. St Peblic was a sixth-century saint who chose his site when Segontium would still have dominated the landscape, though its hour of glory had passed. Of course, the old fort would have been a convenient stone quarry for any building work that Peblic had in mind. *Llanbeblic* – the Church of Peblic – is the name of the parish which includes the whole of Caernarfon.

After crossing the bridges spanning the Afon Seiont (0.8km) and the track of a dismantled railway, turn right (S) along a path. At a wall corner (1.1km), veer left (SE) across a field to wall steps and a gate (1.3km). Cross the next field to critch-cratch 1 (1.5km), continue to a stile and on to critch-cratch 2 and a council road (1.7km). Turn right (SW) to a farm track (1.9km) and left to face Mynydd Mawr's profile – one that has earned it the nickname of *elephant mountain.*

Cross the council road (2.1km), follow the track SE and NE to a farm road, and S to Llety (2.9km). From the stile south of the house continue across the field to critch-cratches 3 (3.0km), 4 (3.2km) and on, between wall boundaries, to Ysbytty Farm (3.5km). Follow the track SW to a farm road (3.7km), turn left (S) and continue to Plas Glan-yr-afon (4.5km, 2.8ml).

This house dates from the late seventeenth century. Much of it is original including the tall square chimneys, the roof timbers and slates. Internally, there are eighteenth-century ceilings and panelling. The outbuildings are also distinctive.

One continues E along the farm track, feeling that the surroundings too have changed little in a couple of centuries. At a track intersection (5.0km) turn right (S) down to a bridge spanning the sparkling Afon Gwyrfal (5.2km). Here, the feeling of timelessness seems confirmed. Across the bridge, turn left to a stile and follow the path SE up the hill and E alongside the course of a dismantled railway. Turn right (5.4km) across the old railway track and continue southward past Tan-yr-allt (5.5km) to a track intersection (6.0km). Keeping S, follow the path between field walls to critch-cratch 5 (6.3km) and continue up the hill past a wall corner to a council road

(6.6km).

The path lies south-eastward to a wall corner (7.2km) where one has a feeling of liberation at last now that open spaces lie ahead. Continue S past the heathered mounds of Moelsmytho on the left as the near-profile of elephant mountain comes into view. Beyond the end of the boundary wall (9.7km) the climb up the elephant's knee begins (160°).

Up by the rim of the cwm a hang-glider expert might dream of launching across the precipice and following the course of the Afon Gwynfor towards the sea, skimming across the villages of Betws Garmon and Waunfawr and on to the towers of Caernarfon Castle.

From the edge of the cwm (10.6km) bear 160° to the summit cairn (10.9km, 6.8ml). On a clear day this is a splendid vantage point for taking stock of Eryri. The premier peak itself sits NE across the valley, a citadel with its lesser summits ranged in random order. To the SW is Llyn Nantlleuchaf, the slate quarries and the west coast. To the NW the Anglesey coast recedes into the hazy distance. In the opposite direction (SE), the downward path offers splendid views of peaks, ridges and lakes, S and E round the rim of Cwm Planwydd to the lower summit, Foel Rudd (12.2km).

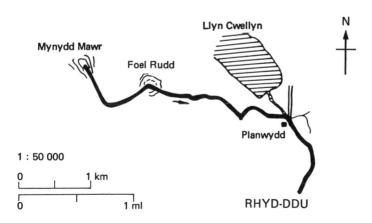

Continuing the descent, Llyn Cwellyn reveals her shape. *Cawell* is a cradle. *Cawellyn*, or *Cwellyn:* cradle lake. There is some doubt as to which side of this cradle-shaped lake the Romans built their road. The south-west side would have offered the shorter route but it would probably have been more vulnerable to attack than the NE side. A Roman residence is said to have occupied the site where the Castle Cidwn Hotel now stands.

At the third stile (14.0km), turn NE into the plantation, descend to the forestry station Planwydd (14.9km) and turn right to Rhyd-ddu (16.0km, 10ml).

Rhyd-ddu

Rhyd means ford, *du* or *ddu* gloomy. *Rhyd-ddu:* gloomy ford. Perhaps this suggests an unpromising beginning at a time when names were being attached to places. More recent history has certainly redeemed this village's reputation.

Here it stands near the foot of Snowdon where climbers set off for a world-famous summit. Here it was that one of Wales's literary giants, T. H. Parry-Williams (1889–1975), was born. He won the National Eisteddfod crown and chair in the same year twice – 1912 in Wrexham and 1915 in Bangor – and he always took an opportunity to acknowledge Rhyd-ddu and its surroundings as being a primary source of his inspiration as a poet and essayist. In his poem *Moelni* – Bareness – he described how he responded to his boyhood environment.

> Nid oedd ond llymder anial byd di-goed
>   O gylch fy ngeni yn Eryri draw,
> Fel petai'r cewri wedi bod erioed
>   Yn hir lyfnhau'r llechweddau ar bob llaw;
> A thros fy magu, drwy flynyddoedd syn
>   Bachgendod yn ein cartref uchel ni,
> Ymwasgai henffurf y mynyddoedd hyn,
>   Nes mynd o'u moelni i mewn i'm hanfod i.

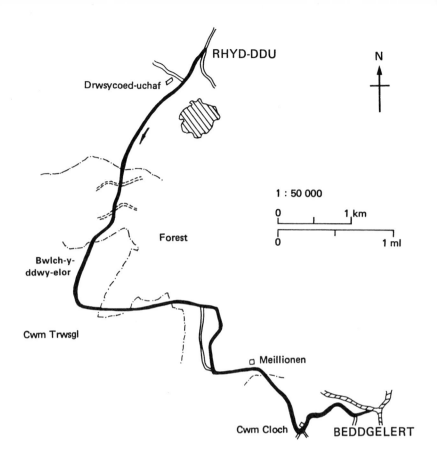

Only sharpness reigned in the treeless world
    Round my birthplace in Snowdonia yonder,
As if the giants had ever been
    Relentlessly grinding the slopes on all sides;
And while growing up, through wondering years
    Of boyhood in our upland home,
The age-old form of these mountains encroached,
    Until it thrust deep into my soul.

At the village school is a museum displaying the life and work of the bard. Entering it and imbibing its messages is a fitting preparation for enjoying the romance of the bard's country.

Rhyd-ddu – Beddgelert: 10.3km, 6.4ml.

Follow the Nantlle road for 400m and continue along the path, bearing 240°, passing the eighteenth-century farmhouse, Drwsycoed-uchaf, on the right. From the forest boundary (1.9km) the path continues for about 200m where it is obliterated at a forest road intersection. Continue southward (200°) along the forest road to another intersection, turn right (220°) and, after 40m, left (210°) onto a path. It winds up past a disused quarry to *Bwlch-y-ddwy-elor:* gap of the two biers. Such must have been the impression of the two mounds to those who gave this bwlch its name.

After passing a gate (3.4km) fork left down through an old slate quarry, veer to S (4.0km), and SE (4.1km), between rugged mounds that signal one's arrival in *Cwm Trwsgl* – Cwm of Difficulty. The difficulty, whatever it was, seems to have given way to a surfeit of rugged beauty.

Continue E over a wall stile into the Beddgelert Forest (4.5km). At the forest road (4.7km) turn left then right and continue E to stiles at the forest boundary (4.9km). The path lies across a stretch of open ruggedness and leads into the plantation again (5.6km). Turn left, then right at the next three forest roads. At the next (6.1km), a turn right takes one S and E to Meillionen. Alternatively, continue to the forest boundary, E past a cottage to a stile (6.4km), turn right and continue for 200m. Fork right (SW) and continue S and E onto a grass path (7.6km) leading to Meillionen farmhouse (8.0km) which dates from the seventeenth century.

Bear SE from the yard to a corner wall-stile (8.2km), continue to a forest road (8.3km) and on to critch-cratch 7 (8.6km) at the edge of the forest. Turn right (S/SE) and follow the farm road to Cwm Cloch (9.3km), another farmhouse dating from the seventeenth century. Continue along the farm road for a further 200m, turn right over a stream and fork left (060°) along a track which turns SE between field walls and leads to a stile (9.9km). Bear E into Beddgelert (10.3km, 6.4ml).

Beddgelert

Eliminating the possibility of attack from hilltops by local Ordovices would have been urgent for the Romans in order to assure their safe passage through these passes. Dinas Emrys (map ref: 606492) offered the most significant threat.

This strategic hill at the southern end of Llyn Dinas had been occupied for countless centuries before the Romans arrived, and was to be used after their departure up to about the twelfth century. It was a function of Pen-y-gwryd, the Roman camp down the valley beyond Nantgwynant, to provide the power for keeping Dinas Emrys, and all the lesser strongpoints in the area, neutralised.

After the occupation there remained on the site of Beddgelert an isolated Celtic community, among whom rose a priory, the oldest in Wales apart from the one on Bardsey Island. The monastery carried on an independent existence up to about 1200 when it came under the authority of the Abbey of Aberconwy. This was the period when the Parish Church of St Mary was founded. Of the thirteenth-century Priory Chapel there remains the north wall, including the doorway to the vestry, two fine arches dividing the nave from the transeptal chapel, and the east wall with its beautiful triplet lancet window.

Bedd refers to a grave, *gelert* derives from a sixth-century St Giler. This man's story is lost in the mists of time, which was very convenient for the eighteenth-century originator of that other gelert, Llywelyn the Great's faithful hound, whose fable can scarcely be missed in Beddgelert. Less well known is the authentic historical presence of Wales's most popular hero: Owain Glyndwr (1359–1416).

At the beginning of the fifteenth century an air of violent conflict pervaded the British Isles. King Richard II had been overthrown in 1399 by an armed seizure of power and Henry IV was installed in his place. England was waging intermittent war in France, in Ireland and against the Scots. In 1400, Wales blazed into revolt when the Lord Marcher in north

Wales, Lord Grey of Ruthin, sought to arrest Owain Glyndwr for ostensibly refusing to respond to the king's summons for service against the Scots. Glyndwr escaped and succeeded in uniting almost the whole of Wales. Indeed, he was proclaimed Prince of Wales by his followers. He summoned a parliament and concluded a treaty with the King of France. But he was confronted by superior forces. During a period of defeat, about the year 1406, Glyndwr used, near Beddgelert, a cave which has been known ever since as Ogof Owain Glyndwr (map ref: 562478). A traditional story relates that supplies for the rebel chieftain were organised by the Prior of Beddgelert.

The cave is at the far end of Cwm Meillionen, in a rugged outcrop beneath the summit of Moel Hebog. From this vantage point lookouts could keep the entire surrounding areas under surveillance, as far as the peak of Snowdon, which rises magnificently across the valley.

The insurrection which Glyndwr led ended in defeat but after six centuries his memory remains undimmed; not least in Beddgelert.

Beddgelert – Nantmor – Croesor – Maentwrog – Gellilydan Tomen-y-mur: 19.5km, 12.2ml.

From the bridge spanning the Afon Colwyn (00km), bear W along the A498 and fork right by the Royal Goat Hotel over the stile used on the way into the village. Follow the path (250°) to a gate (0.6km), through a wall opening (0.7km) and SW to a wall gate (0.9km). Cross the farm road and continue SW up the field to a gated opening (1.0km) between two plantations. On a general bearing S find the way to the top of the ridge (1.4km).

Here is a place to look back at Beddgelert, compact in its valley junction; and across to Snowdon (030°) whose southern ridge stands out sharply on a clear day.

Continue downhill (S) to the valley bottom and on across rough pasture, keeping S then SE, to Oerddwr-uchaf (2.6km), sheltering below the crags, with its waterwheel giving one the

rebel and prior

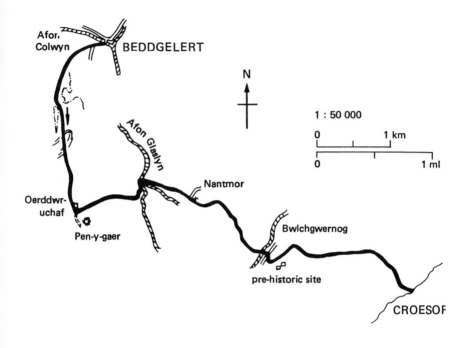

impression of a self-sufficient hill farm generating its own power supply.

What appears as a volcanic top lies about 300m distant on a bearing of 150°. This is Pen-y-gaer, the site of a pre-historic fort. Eastwards, there is a view of Nantmor village, appearing to huddle at the feet of the Cnicht and the Moelwyns.

On reaching a gate (3.3km) in the boundary wall of the Aberglaslyn Woods there is the delight of entering a natural deciduous woodland. Descend along a walled path down to the A498 (3.9km), turn left to the Aberglaslyn bridge (4.0km) and, 30m beyond it along the Penrhyndeudraeth road to the left, climb onto a ledge-path which leads past Pen-y-groes cottage (4.3km) and on to Nantmor chapel (4.8km, 3ml).

Nantmor

A secluded haven in a leafy upland within close reach of the Pass of Aberglaslyn. This is how it may have appeared to those substantial citizens of long ago who built houses here.

Ty-mawr, otherwise known as *Capel Anwes* – chapel of ease (map ref: 610462) – which dates from the fifteenth century, and since that time a notable house in the parish of Beddgelert.

Hafod Garegog (map ref: 604444) dates from about 1600 when it replaced an earlier mansion. The site includes a mill, a cottage and a barn, all of the seventeenth century.

Gardd-llygaid-y-dydd – garden of daisies (map ref: 605457) – dates from the early seventeenth century.

Nantmor, or *Nanmor*, derives from *Nant-y-mor* gorge or brook by the sea, which washed up close to this place in earlier times.

Occupation in pre-historic times has been confirmed by the discovery of stone and bronze tools, and by the remains of stone huts and enclosures. Whether any Romans settled here we do not know but one certainly has a feeling of their presence along the way ahead.

Continue eastwards from the chapel. By tradition, this is the route of the Roman road. The tradition acquires a feeling of reality after crossing the council road at Bwlchwernog (6.1km) onto a track that leads S up the hill to a gate (6.3km), then veers E/NE. However, this route is of greater antiquity than the Roman period. To the SE, about 200m, is the site of a pre-historic settlement known as *Cytiau Gwyddelod* – huts of the Irish (map ref: 614451).

Tramping through all this splendid ruggedness one has a feeling that the Romans might have departed only yesterday along the track to Croesor. But, suddenly, we *are* in Croesor (8.5km, 5.3ml).

Croesor

Here is the small village that climbers seek as a base from which to tackle the Cnicht and the Moelwyns. It occupies an ancient site associated with that legendary figure, Helen. Who exactly was that woman whose name has been bestowed upon the arterial Roman roads of Snowdonia? Here, there is *Ffynnon Helen* – Helen's spring – on the very edge of the village. It has been said that Helen's army rested by it: What campaign was she engaged in? Was she a Snowdonia Boadicea? – a chieftess of the Ordovices? The idea is attractive. If true we could reasonably expect a clearer record of her life, and we might delight in a celebration of her inspiration. Or, has her legend derived from St Helena (died 338 AD), mother of the Emperor Constantine? – she may have been the daughter of a British/Celtic chieftain.

Croesor refers to a cross or border. The names round about suggest that here was some kind of frontier between provinces. In the locality one senses that kind of feeling. Head up Cwm Croesor between the Cnicht and the Moelwyns and enter a remote world where self can feel itself.

Continue SE up the hill over Pont Maesgwm (9.3km). At the top of the hill, just before entering the plantation (9.6km), is the spot to take one's leave of Croesor, nestling in the mouth of its cwm beneath the tower of the Cnicht.

We now pass into the Vale of Ffestiniog. Ahead is a view of ridges arranged like a series of backdrops to the action in the valley below. Such action may be revealed in the form of a shrill sound from a locomotive whistle.

Turn left over a stile (9.9km) and through critch-cratch 1 to a bridge spanning the railway track at Tan-y-bwlch station. There, an incredible locomotive may be hissing and puffing in its resplendent brasses.

legendary Helen

Continue SW from the station, turn sharp left (SE) along the B4410 for 400m to critch-cratch 2 and a forest road on the right (W). Follow the forest road which winds above attractive Llyn Mair. At 11.4km, just beyond a forest gate, one may veer left onto a path (E) which leads down to the lake shore, rejoining the forest road at 11.7km.

At the forest road junction, turn right (SW) and follow SE to join the Plas Tan-y-bwlch drive (12.2km). Here is one of the most significant houses in Snowdonia, historically and architecturally. It is a successor of earlier houses that represented the centre of an estate extending over a wide area from Llanfrothen to Dolwyddelan. In the sixteenth century the incumbent squire was a descendant of the Welsh Prince Gruffydd ap Cynan. Here was a meeting place for Welsh bards where literary talents were fostered and generous hospitality provided. In the eighteenth century, a daughter married a William Oakley from Staffordshire. In the house of poets, a new departure was initiated: into quarrying, land improvement and architecture. The Oakleys were not mere seekers of wealth. They were aesthetes who pursued artistic excellence. They practised their arts and crafts in this valley, especially upon the village of Maentwrog.

Turn left (NE) and follow the drive down to the A487 (12.6km) and across the Afon Dwyryd to Maentwrog (13.2km).

Maentwrog

Look at the long blocks of stone, all carefully shaped to fit exactly into place. It would seem that mortar is scarcely necessary for these exquisitely designed buildings.

The concept was that of William Oakley's son, William Griffith Oakley (1790–1835), whose basic theme was harmony with the surroundings. A true artist, he spared no effort to achieve satisfying creations. He personally supervised extraction of the types of stone he wished to see used in construc-

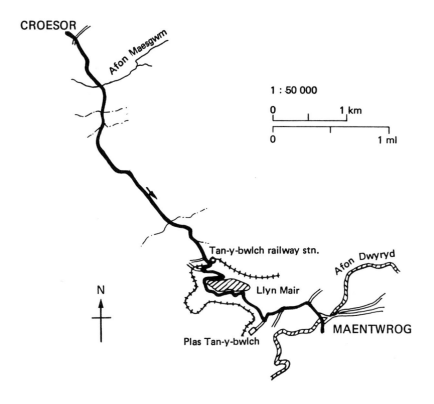

CROESOR

Afon Maesgwm

1 : 50 000

0   1 km

0   1 ml

Tan-y-bwlch railway stn.

Afon Dwyryd

N

Llyn Mair

MAENTWROG

Plas Tan-y-bwlch

tion. He was succeeded by his nephew, William Edward
Oakley (1828–1912), who carried on his uncle's work.

Maentwrog is as fortunate in its topography as it has
been in its history. High land to the south and east, and low
river plain to the north and west preclude the type of development that would spoil this attractive village.

In the churchyard, among three large yew trees which
are reputably more than 1000 years old, W. E. Oakley lies
with his wife and son under three Celtic headstones. Across
the valley is Plas Tan-y-bwlch, with its beautifully land-
scaped gardens and the Ffestiniog Railway passing behind,
now a National Park Study Centre. One feels that the Oakleys
would have enthusiastically approved of the way in which

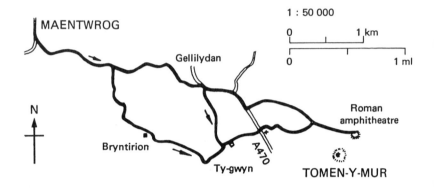

their old home is being used, for their taste for artistic creation extended to encouraging all types of educational activity.

Fork left along the council road 50m from the Maentwrog PO and climb the hill with the prospect of alternative routes ahead. The first alternative is to pass to the south of Gellilydan by turning right (14.6km) along a farm road past Nant-y-March to Bryntirion (17.3km), south-eastward through a succession of gates to a stile (18.3km) and E past the farmhouse Ty-gwyn.

But the Roman road must, surely, have passed through Gellilydan (16.0km) where one looks for some kind of monument; not to the Romans but to the victory of the Welsh Prince, Gruffydd ap Cynan (1055–1137). As ruler of Gwynedd, it was he who achieved what Wales should have every right to commemorate: a Welsh defeat of the Normans who, not long previously, had conquered the Saxons.

Gellilydan . . . . and Gruffydd ap Cynan

Gruffydd had been tricked by the Normans into attending a conference, was seized and thrown into Chester prison where he remained for some years. After making his escape he roused Gwynedd and marched into the border lands of England. In 1095, William Rufus (King William II) decided to put down this troublesome foe before the winter closed in. He advanced into Gwynedd but was harried by Gruffydd with guerrilla tactics. The vital encounter occurred here within sight of Tomen-y-mur where Rufus had encamped. Gruffydd sent the invader scurrying back to Chester, gaining for Wales almost a couple of centuries of independence.

South-east along the A487 for 1km, turn left (E) and 1.8km further on is the site of the Roman fort.

To take a route by path from Gellilydan, continue SE from the PO (16.0km) and fork right by the bridge (16.4km). Follow the path S to a stile (16.7km); 200m further on veer SW through woodland to a wall stile (17.2km) and on to a stile by a farm track (17.4km). Turn left and continue E past Ty-gwyn (17.6km) across the A487 (18.0km) to a gate by a chapel. After crossing a bridge that spans a railway track, veer right over a stile, left (E) to a gated opening by a barn, right (SE) and then left (E). The motte on top of Tomen-y-mur, built by William Rufus during his campaign against Gruffydd, comes into view (SE) as one climbs the hill alongside a slated fence. At the council road (18.7km), turn right (SE) and continue to the Roman amphitheatre (19.5km, 12.2ml).

Tomen-y-mur

Here was a road junction. South-eastward, near the SW end of Bala lake, lay the fort of Caer Gai. Southwards, there were at least two forts on the road to Moridunum (Carmarthen).

Tomen-y-mur was a pivotal fort, the southern corner of a network which encompassed Snowdonia. It was established about 78 AD as part of Agricola's conquest of north Wales. The fort was run down as Roman rule became consolidated and other commitments assumed greater priority. Occupation ended about 130–140.

Beyond the SE gate was a bath-house and there was also a civilian settlement. But there were special features not found in other Snowdonia forts. One was the amphitheatre, 350m NE of the fort. It would hardly have been used as a venue for amateur dramatics; most likely it was a site for demonstrating combat techniques. At Dolddinas, about 2.4km SE, there were camps. Both these features seem to suggest intensive training. As a cross-roads site, Tomen-y-mur could have served the entire region in what must have been a necessary aid to morale on this far-western frontier of empire.

Excavations in 1962 showed that the fort had begun as a four-acre site but was reduced to approximately three acres about the year 120. It is known that preparations were then proceeding in the north for the building of Hadrian's Wall and it is possible that Roman rule was well enough consolidated by then to allow a partial reduction of forces.

A thousand years after the fort was established, William Rufus left his mark on it in the form of a motte, a mound about 30ft high. Perhaps he intended to build a castle. If he did the project was cut short by Gruffydd ap Cynan who put the Norman forces to flight.

Turning northward from Tomen-y-mur towards the Roman fort in the Llugwy Valley, Caer Llugwy, near Betws-y-coed, across parts of Snowdonia that have remained remote

and retained a unique *feeling* of Eryri, we shall encounter positively identified remains of Roman road. The ancient trackways that the Romans used, and the parts of Roman road that were available to packhorsemen, were all inherited by slate quarrymen who travelled between home and work on foot.

Tomen-y-mur – Caer Llugwy: 23.1km, 14.5ml

Tomen-y-mur – Dolwyddelan: 16.3km, 10.2ml.

From the amphitheatre (00km) walk northward near the forest boundary to the corner of the second plantation area (0.9km). Bear NE to a stile (1.3km) and continue through the plantation to a stile at the plantation boundary (1.7km). Cross the stream, passing the house Llech Goronwy on the right, and follow the forest road downhill past the farmhouse Bryn-saeth (2.2km) to the road junction (2.6km).

After crossing the Afon Cynfal, turn right (030°) and follow the council road to the B4391. Cross the road, veer left and continue northward along the farm road past the Water Board station (4.9km). Around the hill to the right is Bryn y Castell which once served the Romans as an observation post guarding the southern end of the pass. Fork left (5.5km) and, 100m further on, veer left. The Roman route bears N and NE to *Rhyd yr Helen* – Helen's ford. Here is another monument to that mysterious woman whose name leaves us intensely curious.

The route of the Roman road bears generally 030° along a ridge between two valleys. On the left is the massive mound of Manod Mawr; on the right is a succession of knolls. Peace reigns; a feeling of tranquillity descends. Here is remoteness painted in rugged colours.

On reaching the head of the pass the agger of the Roman road can be seen. The road may be followed through the plantation to the boundary of the disused Rhiwbach slate quarry

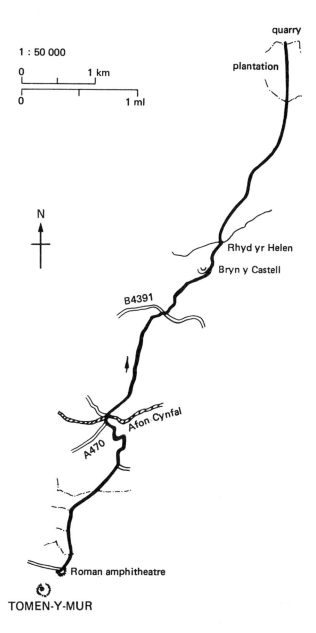

1 : 50 000

0   1 km

0   1 ml

N

quarry

plantation

Rhyd yr Helen

Bryn y Castell

B4391

Afon Cynfal

A470

Roman amphitheatre

TOMEN-Y-MUR

(8.9km). From the northern side of the quarry bear 340° across a magnificent wilderness that gives birth to the Afon Machno which issues in myriad trickles into its own valley where it meanders along to join the Conwy.

From the next plantation boundary (10.7km) the track down through Cwm Penamnen is best known as a quarry-men's path though it was also the route of a packhorse trail. Three forest roads are crossed before reaching *Ty'n-y-cwm* – house in the cwm (12.8km). The cottage *Tan-y-bwlch* – under the gap (13.4km) – lies at the lower end of an old packhorse trail that winds westward up the side of the cwm and on to Roman Bridge in the Lledr Valley. On the right is the farm-house *Gwyndy-newydd* – new white house – *new* because it once replaced a seventeenth-century house further up the cwm.

Continue to Pentre-bont and Dolwyddelan (16.3km, 10.2ml).

Dolwyddelan

Dol means meadow. *Dolwyddelan,* or colloquially, *Dol'ddelan,* refers to Gwyddelan's meadow. He was one of those sixth-century saints whose names are immortalised in the places they settled.

The Parish Church of St Gwyddelan is 100m SE along the Pentre-bont road from the post office. It dates from about 1500 when it replaced an earlier church 300m to the SW on a hill called *Bryn y Bedd* – hill of the tomb. From the post office walk 350m W along the A470 and turn left through a pair of iron gates up to the cemetery. This is a point from which Gwyddelan must have viewed this large green meadow with its unfailing water supply and rich pasture. On the right is the river, much as it must have been in his day; but there is now the Llandudno to Ffestiniog railway and the remains of slate quarrying. On the left is the main road.

Nowadays, only one road passes through Dolwyddelan,

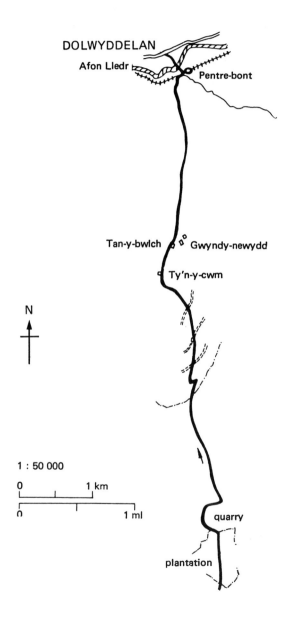

DOLWYDDELAN

Afon Lledr

Pentre-bont

Tan-y-bwlch

Gwyndy-newydd

Ty'n-y-cwm

N

1 : 50 000

0   1 km

0   1 ml

quarry

plantation

59

along the valley of the Afon Lledr, but when travel was by foot and packhorse, this meadow was the nodal point in a path network connecting many scattered mountain communities. Fortunately, these paths, traced out over thousands of years, remain for our use. They make this village an ideal centre for exploring a wide area of Snowdonia.

Dolwyddelan – Caer Llugwy: 6.8km, 4¹/₄ml.

The Roman route through the Lledr Valley is generally supposed to lie north-eastward near Pont-y-pant.

From Dolwyddelan PO walk SE over Pont y Llan, fork left past the school and follow the farm road along the river bank to Pont-y-pant railway station (3km, 1.9ml). Continue to the bridge Pont-y-pant and climb the hill to join Sarn Helen which leads NE through the deserted village of Rhiwddolion (5.6km, 3.6ml) to the hamlet of Pentre-du (6.3km, 4ml) by the A5 in the Llugwy Valley. This is well to the east of Caer Llugwy which may, nevertheless, be reached by following paths westward along the northern side of the river past *Rhaeadr Gwennol* (Swallow Falls) and *Ty-hyll* (The Ugly House). It seems, therefore, that Caer Llugwy was not situated at a crossroads. It lay on a route westward through the Llugwy Valley to Pen-y-gwryd and Segontium.

A more direct route to the Roman fort may be taken by following a packhorse trail.

From the Dolwyddelan PO (00km) follow the village lane NW up the hill for 100m, turn right through critch-cratch 1 and, 50m further on, veer left to critch-cratch 2 (0.3km).

Continue to a forest road (0.8km), turn left (N), take the left fork at 1.2km and avoid all turnings to left or right until reaching the boundary forest gate (3.2km). The trail crosses moorland at the foot of Moel-siabod, then winds NW down into the Llugwy Valley. On the descent there is a striking view of Cyfyng Falls (330°) cascading beneath Cyfyng Bridge which provides access from the A5 to the hamlet of Pont Cyfyng.

On reaching a council road (5.7km), turn right (E) along

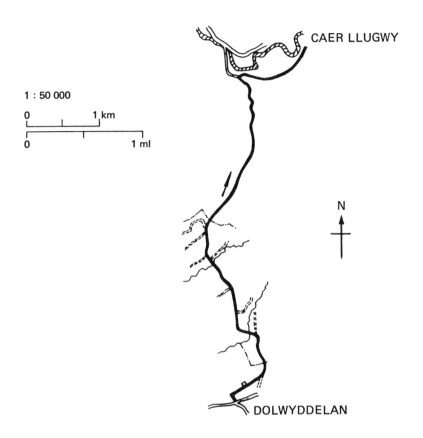

what was almost certainly the Roman route from Segontium and Pen-y gwryd to Caer Llugwy (6.8km, 4¹/₄ml).

Caer Llugwy

A day's march between forts seems to have been a principle of Roman military planning. Caer Llugwy provided an intermediate site between Tomen-y-mur and Canovium but that was not its sole purpose. There had to be a direct link through Snowdonia with Segontium. In pre-historic times there was a trackway along the Llugwy and Nantygwryd valleys and through the Llanberis Pass. The marching camp at Pen-y-gwryd shows that the Romans used this route.

Caer Llugwy was ideally sited on the eastern side of the mountains near the valley junction where Betws-y-coed now stands. It fitted neatly into a loop of the Afon Llugwy which almost encircled it on three sides – an aid to defence.

The fort was a little less than four acres and there was an annexe of just over three acres. It seems to have been founded later than the other Snowdonia forts – about 100 AD – but occupation continued until Tomen-y-mur was evacuated.

Excavations have shown that metal-smelting was carried on here. The name *Bryn-y-gefeilia* – hill of smithies – may well have originated in Roman times.

Caer Llugwy – Canovium: 21.3km, 13.3ml

Caer Llugwy – Llanrhychwyn – Trefriw: 9.7km, 6ml.

From the gate at Caer Llugwy field (00km), bear 060° along the council road to the A5 (1.2km) and turn left over the bridge. The fifteenth-century *Ty-hyll* – Ugly House – is 50m along the road. By tradition, it is a *ty nos* – a house of the night – built, according to an old custom, between sunset and sunrise, when smoke rising from the chimney secured the property for its builder. With some of the massive stones weighing more than two tons, that was an incredible feat!

After crossing the bridge turn right (E) and follow the path along the bank of the river to *Rhaeadr-ewynol* – the foaming fall (Swallow Falls) – where the Afon Llugwy displays its finest white plumage as it cascades down the gorge. The path slices along the cliff face high above the river to a stream (2.9km) flowing down from Llyn Ty'n-y-mynydd reservoir, and then to another, 250m further on, cascading from Llyn Pencraig. Continue up through the plantation to a

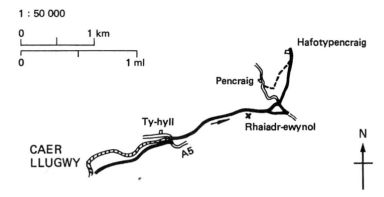

forest road (3.2km), turn sharp left (NW) and, 100m further on, veer right (NE) to a council road (3.4km). (For an alternative path, now partially obscured by the plantation, veer left between the two streams and cross a footbridge to the council road). Cross the road to a stile and continue NE and N to a stile at the forest boundary (3.8km). Fork right, continue N to a stile (4.0km) and on to Hafotypencraig (4.3km, 2.7ml).

This farmhouse is, of course, the *hafod* or *foty* – the summer dwelling - of Pencraig which is down the valley (SW), a walking distance of about half a mile. Sitting snugly against a hillside at the end of a long and beautiful ascent from Pont-y-pair, Betws-y-coed, Pencraig is host to one of the most intriguing stories of old Eryri.

In the early sixteenth century, the tenant was a William Owen, an accomplished harpist, well-known throughout the district as a singer and composer. His most renowned composition was a piece called *Conset*, popularly entitled *Conset William Owen Pencraig.*

Owen's notoriety was not confined to music. He was an agitator for the cause of Wales and, at a time when his country was being drawn more closely under English domination, he was obliged to flee from his home. Of course, he took his harp with him to sustain him on his journeys.

Where he travelled is not recorded. Several years passed without a word reaching Pencraig of his fate. His wife concluded that he must have died and she decided to accept another man's proposal of marriage.

63

On the night before the wedding, Mrs Owen, with her husband-to-be, hosted a nuptial feast. As the parlour filled with guests, a maid told her mistress that there was a strange harpist at the kitchen door. Should she let him in? Pencraig was well known for generous hospitality, not least to wandering harpists who turned up out of the blue. The maid was told to make the man comfortable and give him whatever food and drink he required.

When the stranger had finished refreshing himself he took up his harp. As the chords of *Conset* reached Mrs Owen she left her guests. Standing in the kitchen doorway she recognised the man. What could she say?

She decided to lead her betrothed man into a trap. She told him she had lost the key to Pencraig many years ago and now she was about to have a new one. But the old key had suddenly turned up and she thought it fitted better. What would he advise her to do? He said if the old key suited better, of course she should stick to it and not bother with the new one. She said she would accept his advice.

As the strains of *Conset* subdued the guests she led the luckless man to the kitchen and introduced her husband.

Hafotypencraig has the distinction of not having an access for motor vehicles from the road. The last regular occupants in the 1960s made their way by traditional mode: in a gig pulled by a Welsh mountain pony.

The track they travelled is our way ahead.

Follow the track N to a council road (4.7km), turn right then left (4.8km) along a forest road and left again 100m further on.

Continue northward past the reservoir Llyn Glangors, which nestles scenically into the forested hills, below on the left. At 6.4km a path leads down to the lake.

Fork left at 6.6km and 500m further on veer left again onto a path (350°) that winds northward past slate quarry heaps, offering splendid glimpses over the Conwy Valley. The path joins a farm road at Tan-yr-Eglwys (7.9km). *Tan* means under; *Tan-yr-Eglwys:* under the Church.

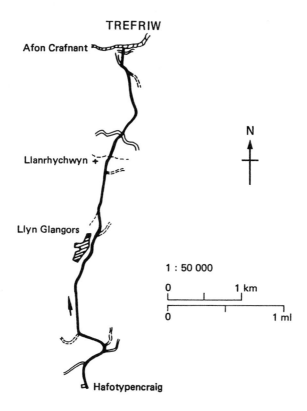

TREFRIW

Afon Crafnant

Llanrhychwyn

Llyn Glangors

N

1 : 50 000

0   1 km

0   1 ml

Hafotypencraig

Llanrhychwyn

It is the ancient Church of Llanrhychwyn 300m up the hill, the Church of Prince Llywelyn ap Iorwerth where he and his wife, Joan, came to worship before the Trefriw Church was built in 1230. In Llywelyn's time it was about half its present size forming approximately a double square around the font, which is said to be the oldest in Britain. With later extensions and alterations the Church reached its present design in the eighteenth century. Services are held on the last Sunday in each month from May to September. The season is concluded with a harvest festival.

Continue from Tan-yr-Eglwys past the road junction (8.3km) and northward along the high bank of the Conwy Valley to a point above Trefriw where a path forks right (040°), past a chapel (N) to a footbridge spanning the Afon Crafnant (9.7km).

Trefriw – Llanbedr-y-cennin – Canovium: 11.6km, 7¹/₄ml.

Continuing from the footbridge (00km), turn left at the next road, sharp right at the next, then left. Fork right along the Cowlyd road (0.2km) and, 100m further on, turn right (NE) up a forest road. At 0.6km fork left (340°), follow the forest road northward to 1.3km and on round a U-bend for about another 60m. Turn sharp right (330°) up a forest path to a stile (1.5km), cross the stream, follow the path up past a slate quarry heap on the left and on (020°) to a stile (1.6km). Cross a field (350°) and continue along a bank into another belt of forest (1.8km). Bear N over a low wall, uphill to a wall corner and along a fence, veering left, to a council road (2.4km).

Turn right (N), passing the hamlet of Rhibo, 100m further on, and continue along the road, which becomes a track, to the ruin of Tyddyn Wilym (3.4km). Bear N and follow a stream path down to an iron footbridge which spans the Afon Ddu (3.6km, 2¹/₄ml). Up through the forest (340°) to a clearing, veer to 350° across a track from the ruined village of Ardda (*Tai-isaf-ardda* – the lower houses of Ardda) on the left (3.9km).

The village of Ardda, and its field systems, covered an area of about 1000m from NE to SW and 500m from NW to SE. A community of interdependent, but independent, upland dwellers lived a self-sufficient life isolated from the valleys and towns. Abandonment began in the late eighteenth century but some residents remained until the 1920s.

Continue up the hill (355°) to a channel which flows down the cwm from Cowlyd (SW), that solitary serene lake

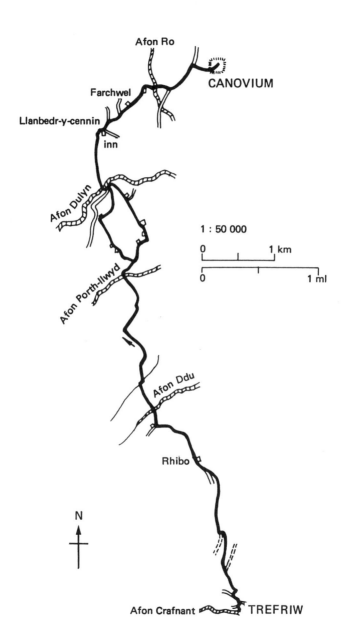

Afon Ro

CANOVIUM

Farchwel

Llanbedr-y-cennin

inn

Afon Dulyn

Afon Porth-llwyd

Afon Ddu

Rhibo

1 : 50 000

| 0 | 1 km |

| 0 | 1 ml |

N

Afon Crafnant

TREFRIW

set between ridges sketched against the sky. Turn right to a footbridge (4.2km). Continue uphill (N) to a disused tram track (4.4km). Follow the tram track NE and N to a footbridge over the channel (5.2km) where the path veers downhill (030°) alongside two pipelines to a junction (5.4km). Continue round the CEGB building and NW alongside the pipeline, then under it, to a stile (5.5km).

Into the forest N/NE, downhill N/NW to a stile (5.9km) and uphill, one comes upon a delightful rock pool (6.0km) set between two waterfalls, part of the Afon Porth-llwyd plunging down to the Conwy and the sea, preparing to supply the Dolgarrog aluminium works with energy. This is a place for a refreshing drink of crystal-clear water.

Join the path along the north bank and follow it E and NE to a stile (6.5km). Turn left (NW) up the track, passing Llidiard-fadog (7.0km) on the left. Fifty metres further up turn right (340°) past a pair of cottages and continue through field wall openings to Carreg-y-ffordd (7.5km). *Carreg* means stone, *ffordd* road. *Carreg-y-ffordd:* stone of road, or roadstone.

Turn through a field gate about 50m from the house and continue downhill (E veering to NE) to a fence corner (7.8km), then N through a belt of forest to a council road (8.2km).

(For an alternative route across terrain, at a lower level, continue from the stile (6.5km) downhill for about 20m, turn left (N) into the woods and follow the path to the cottage Hengae. A farm track descends eastward, then northward, past Bron Haul to Ty-newydd. Turn left through the field gateway by the track to a stream crossing behind the house and continue (340°) over three stiles to Tan'r-allt. Follow the council road uphill for about 400m to an S-bend).

Turn left from the S-bend and 25m up the hill veer right onto a path which winds down to a footbridge that spans the Afon Dulyn (8.4km). About 150m uphill from the bridge one passes Pennant on the left and then along a gentle slope downhill there is a splendid expanse of the lower Conwy. But first, the Bull Inn, Llanbedr-y-cennin (9.4km, 5.9ml).

From the Bull Inn bear N along the Ro-wen road for 400m, veer right (NE) along a farm road to a stile (10.0km), on to another (10.2km) and to the farmhouse, Farchwel. Here is one of the oldest houses in the Conwy Valley, dating from the sixteenth century. It was a good place to build a farm-house, on rich pasture with the Afon Ro flowing through the lower fields. There have been extensive alterations in more than four hundred years but much of the old Farchwel remains, most notably in sixteenth and seventeenth-century woodwork.

Continue along the path to the B5106, turn left and follow the road for 400m to a turning right which is the drive-way along to the Caerhun Church and the site of the Roman fort of Canovium.

Along the Trails of the Packhorse Drivers

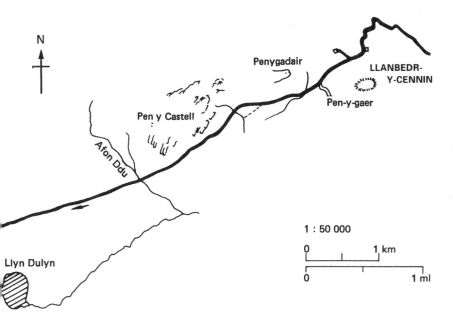

Llanbedr-y-cennin –Tal-y-bont, Llandegai: 21km, 13.2ml

Packhorse drivers set out from Llanbedr across the Carneddau range for Talybont, Llandegai and Bangor.

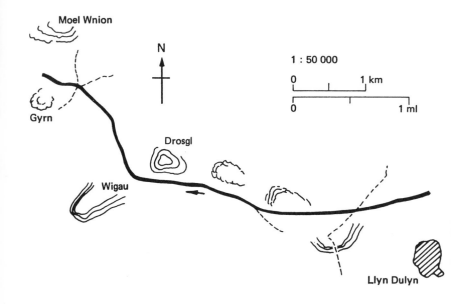

From the Bull Inn (00km), walk W and NW up the hill to a fork left (1.6km) that leads S and W past the old Roman observation post of Pen-y-gaer (elevation 386m, 1268ft) where remains of Roman occupation and fortification may be observed.

Continue past the farm cottage, *Tan-y-gaer* (1.9km) – under the fort – and turn W past *Bron-y-gader* (2.2km) – on the breast of Pen-y-gadair (elevation 496m, 1626ft). *Pen* means head or top; *gadair* or *cadair* means chair. *Pen-y-gadair:* top of the chair. There is a tale that the Celts used to sit on this height observing the Roman lookouts lower down on Pen-y-gaer.

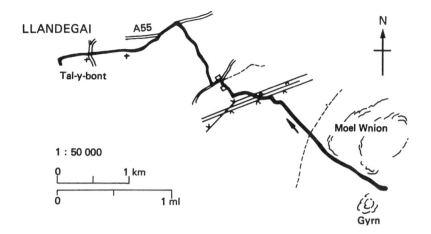

Fork right at 2.7km and 3.0km and follow the old pack-horse trail westward. In various places the trail may be observed as a hollow impression in the ground with rushes growing in it. However, beyond the Afon Ddu ford (5.8km, 3.6ml), there are few remains of the trail and one must bear 250° towards a gap in the ridge, passing the Dulyn reservoir (7.7km) far below on the left.

The ridge (9.0km, 5.6ml; elevation 899m, 2950ft) appears as a place where mountain builders have cast a load of superfluous boulders. They lie about in jagged disarray as if awaiting collection.

After crossing the north-south ridge path the route W lies along the upper edge of Cwm Caseg which sweeps away in a broad expanse down to Bethesda. Between the two mounds Wigau (615m, 2019ft) on the left and Drosgl (757m, 2484ft) on the right (12.3km, 7.7ml), veer NW to a view of the Strait and Anglesey. Remains of the packhorse trail are again in evidence, impressed well down into the hard earth by hooves and feet trudging over countless years.

After passing between Gyrn (542m, 1778ft) on the left and Moel Wnion (580m, 1902ft) on the right, the track descends, crossing the trail from Aber to Rachub (15.5km). Continue to a wall gate (16.5km, 10.3ml), follow the track to another gate (17.2km) and turn right to a council road

(17.6km). Turn left (SW) and, 100m further on, right. Descend to the A55 (18.8km), turn left and, 300m further on, veer left along a council road to a gate by Tal-y-bont Church (20.3km). Continue W along the path to Tal-y-bont village and PO (21km, 13.2ml).

From here the packhorse drivers would have continued to Llandegai and Bangor along a route that is now main road.

Tal-y-bont/Dolgarrog – Capel Curig: 15km, 9.4ml

In the Conwy Valley, Tal-y-bont and Dolgarrog were also starting places for packhorse drivers. This trail leads SW past Llyn Cowlyd, and S to Nant y Benglog and Capel Curig.

Opposite Tal-y-bont PO (00km) a farm track bears SW, turns S, then W (0.2km), to the farmhouse Ty-newydd (450m). Veer left, continue past the house Bron Haul (0.6km) and, 100m further on, turn right (SW) up the track past the cottage Hengae (0.9km). Turn left (S) and follow the path through the woods to a track (1.1km) which rises from the northern end of Dolgarrog.

From Dolgarrog PO, opposite the aluminium works, walk northward along the B5106 for 400m to a lane 50m beyond the bridge spanning the Afon Porthllwyd. Turn left and follow the lane W and S to a gate, then turn right onto a path winding uphill westward.

Continue to a farm road (2.2km) and turn sharp left through a gated opening. The track joins a water channel for a few hundred metres before rejoining the road (2.9km). After crossing the second bridge follow the track up the hill, rising above Coedty reservoir on the right, to a gate near an enclosure (4.5km, 2.8ml).

This track sweeping up the wide cwm at the foot of Moel Eilio (547m, 1793ft), a long ridge on the right, is traditionally regarded as the route of a Roman road; it may have been a

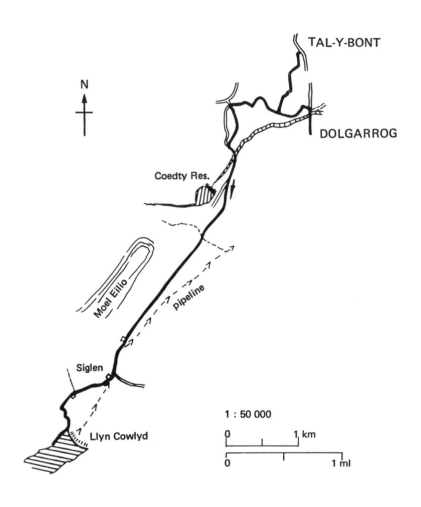

N

TAL-Y-BONT

DOLGARROG

Coedty Res.

Moel Eilio

pipeline

Siglen

Llyn Cowlyd

1 : 50 000

0   1, km

0   1 ml

link between Canovium and the camp at Pen-y-gwryd. Follow the track past the ruin of Pen-bryn-brwynog. *Pen* means top, *bryn* hill, *brwyn* rushes. *Pen-bryn-brwynog:* top of a hill of rushes.

Continue to Siglen, once a most distinguished farmhouse of the Cowlyd area. About 500m further on a path from Llyn Eigiau joins the track near the site of Garreg-wen. Reaching a point above the weir, one can enjoy two magnificent views: down the cwm to the deserted village of Ardda; along the lake

74

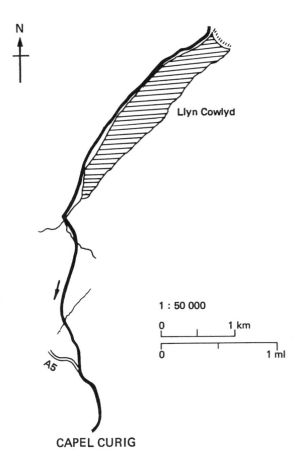

which is gripped between the high masses of Clogwyn Du and Creigiau Gleision.

Follow the track down and veer right (8.3km) along the western shore. There are no boats or vehicles to sully the splendid isolation of this serene mountain lake, only the same pristine purity that inspired a bard who took the name of this lake as his own.

Y llynnau gwyrddion llonydd – a gysgant
   Mewn gwasgod o fynydd,
A thyn heulwen ysblennydd
Ar len y dŵr lun y dydd.

The still blue lakes - they sleep
   In a shelter of mountain,
And a splendid sunlight takes
A picture of the day on the surface of the water.

So wrote Gwilym Cowlyd (Gwilym Roberts, 1828–1904) who was born down the cwm at Tyddyn Wilym, Ardda. Like his uncle, Ieuan Glan Geirionydd, he sang of nature's perfection as he saw it all about him, this inspiring scenery providing the well-spring of his inspiration which brought him fame throughout Wales and beyond.

From the footbridge over Bwlch Cowlyd above the southern end of the lake (11.7km) continue down the broad breast of the Llugwy Valley, flanked by the rugged Glyders higher up to the right, the dark green forests of the lower valley to the left and Siabod's weathercock summit straight ahead. The visibility of Siabod's peak (872m, 2860ft) has long been regarded by people living in the region of these mountains as the surest sign of weather intentions.

After passing the farmhouse Tal-y-waun (13.5km) turn left along the road to Capel Curig (15km, 9.4ml).

Capel Curig is one of Eryri's nodal points: a valley junction and river confluence; and hence an intersection of tracks, trails and paths.

Capel Curig – Bethesda: 18.5km, 11.5ml

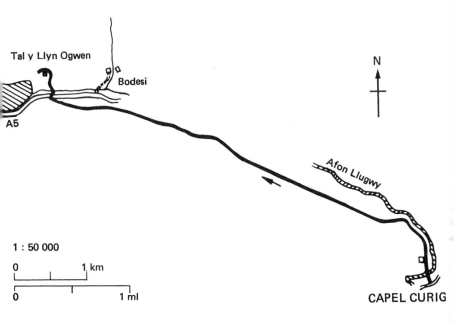

Capel Curig – Pont Pen-y-benglog: 9.2km, 5³/₄ml.

From Capel Curig PO (00km) bear N across the Afon Llugwy, passing Geni on the left (0.3km) and follow the track westward. There is a tradition that this was the route of a Roman road. Certainly, it was a packhorse trail as well as an eighteenth-century road.

In an area rich in legend and folklore, one of the most intriguing stories is that concerning the name *Bodesi*. There is a farmhouse Bodesi (map ref: 676608), an Afon Bodesi and a Pont Bodesi. It is said to derive from Boadicea who is alleged to have fled here from her Roman enemies. Did the great warrior queen inspire Helen, that mysterious woman who still shelters behind an enigmatic veil?

From the critch-cratch by the A5 (6.4km, 4ml), cross the road and follow the path to the north of Tal y Llyn Ogwen (6.9km) and W along the north side of the lake. Ogwen is an

77

artist in mist. If the weather is right the performance can be fascinating as the lake drapes great wispy statues round the rugged peaks.

Under Pont Pen-y-benglog is an intriguing arch of stones, laid as if by a bridge craftsman practising his craft. The stones are said to be from a Roman bridge, taken down when the modern bridge was built, and relaid in an arch beneath it.

A diversion to Llyn Idwal is a journey to the end of the Ice Age, for it was here in this isolated Eryri retreat that a few specimens of Ice Age plants survived the earth's warming process, to be discovered by Edward Lloyd, a late seventeenth-century naturalist and then by Evan Roberts, a local naturalist and warden of the Cwm Idwal nature reserve from 1954, who recorded his discoveries in *Llyfr Rhedyn Ei Daid*.

Llyn Idwal

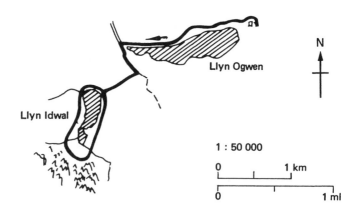

From the Ogwen Cottage Outdoor Centre (00km), follow the path, S, SE, and SW to Llyn Idwal (1.0km). The lake gained its name from Idwal, the murdered son of Prince Owen Gwynedd. Nefydd Hardd, founder of Gwynedd's Fifteen Noble Tribes, was appointed the child's foster father. For

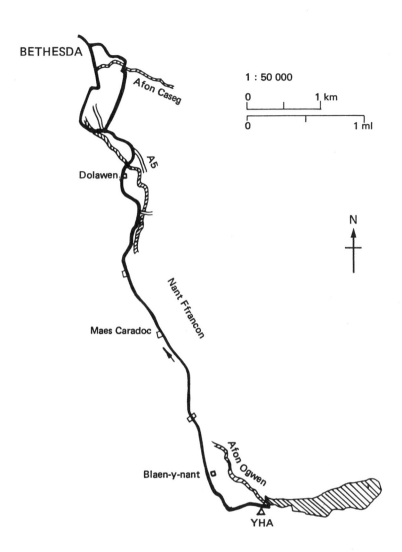

some unknown motive, Nefydd induced his son, Dunawd, to take Idwal into the mountains where, on arriving by this lake, Idwal was killed. The crime was discovered; Nefydd and his family became outcasts. But they were too adept to remain down indefinitely. Rhûn, Nefydd's grandson, retrieved the family standing by becoming an adviser to Owen Gwynedd's grandson, Llywelyn the Great.

Round the lake, almost enclosing it, is a spectacular mountain ring as dramatic as any in Eryri. The place from which to view is high above the southern end from amongst the remains of a pre-historic avalanche where enormous boulders stand as they came to rest.

Ogwen – Bethesda: 9.2km, 5³/₄ml.

From Ogwen Youth Hostel (00km) follow the Old Bethesda Road westward, then northward. This route was once described as "the most dreadful horse-path in Wales." That was before 1791 when Lord Penrhyn, the quarry master, built the first road through Nant Ffrancon to Capel Curig. Penrhyn's road was soon superseded early in the following century by the predecessor of the A5. Thus, this old route was spared from modern over-improvement and it remains a quiet by-way.

At Pont y Ceunant (5.6km, 3¹/₂ml) follow the path northward to Dolawen (6.4km). Cross the bridge to the A5, turn left and, 400m further on, fork eastward or westward. The E route, from the roadside (7.3km), is a path through woodland and a succession of critch-cratches. It joins a path on the right at 8.2km. After passing the next critch-cratch (8.3km), turn left along a lane, right over the road bridge that spans the Afon Caseg, left into the road Abercaseg and continue to the lane alongside the school Ysgol Abercaseg. Turn left at the end of the lane to the A5 and right to the Bethesda PO (9.5km).

To take the W route, from the roadside (7.3km), turn left over the bridge spanning the Afon Ogwen (Pont Ogwen) and follow the path northward above the river bank past Penrhyn Quarry on the left. Cross Pont Twr (8.3km) to the A5 and turn left to the Bethesda PO (9.2km, 5³/₄ml).

Returning to Llyn Ogwen we may follow a trail to another Eryri nodal point: Dolwyddelan.

Llyn Ogwen – Dolwyddelan: 20 km, 12.5ml

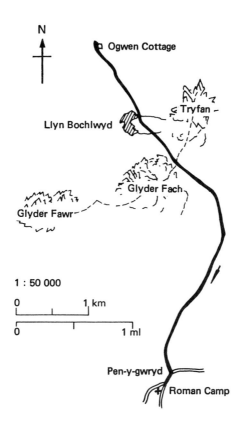

Llyn Ogwen – Pen-y gwryd: 7km, 4.4ml.

From Ogwen Cottage bear SE and climb the jagged bank alongside a waterfall cascading from Llyn Bochlwyd (1.4km). Continue up to the Bristly Ridge (2.4km) between Tryfan (917m, 3008ft) on the left and Glyder Fach (994m, 3262ft) on the right. The route lies south-eastward across slopes of scree facing the wide expanse of Cwm Tryfan, plunging northward to Nant y Benglog on the left.

At the top (3.5km; elevation 762m, 2500ft) there is a grassy plateau that seems to be suspended from the sky. On its southern edge (4.3km) one has an aerial view of the valley junction where the Romans sited their marching camp. The descent towards it (200°) is across a rocky bank covered in places by a rich variety of heathers.

Pen-y-gwryd

The A4086 and A498 join near the centre of the Roman campsite which was rhomboidal in shape with sides 240 yards and 200 yards enclosing an area of about 9¹/₂ acres. The Pen-y-gwryd hotel straddles the camp's northern boundary. Here was the Roman staging post between Bryn-gefeilia in the Llugwy Valley and Segontium by the Menai Strait. Parts of the defences may be observed as a grass-covered bank about three feet high.

Pen-y-gwryd – Dolwyddelan: 13km, 8.1ml.

Depart southwards, about 60 yards west of the Roman gate, to a stile (7.6km) and continue down the track to Gwastadanas (9.6km) where the old house dates from the sixteenth century. Opposite the next farmhouse, Hafod-y-rhisgl, turn left through a gate (10.5km), bear 160° uphill across the A498, 140° to a path that winds up through woods to a wall (11.4km) and on to a fence at the top of the rise (12.0km). Ahead, descending eastward into the Lledr Valley, is a track-way route once used by the ancient Celts.

There is a branch track south-eastward at 12.9km. Further east the track crosses the Afon Diwaunydd (13.9km), flowing from the twin lakes of that name. Continue eastward through a plantation to the ford Ceunant-y-garnedd (15.8km), SE to Ffridd (16.4km), E to Penrhiw farm (17.4km) and on to Dolwyddelan Castle (18.5km).

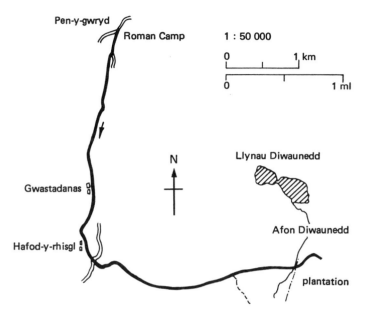

Approaching the castle at eye-level from the west, one may sense some of the romantic mystery of this hilltop sentinel. It dates from the end of the twelfth century, but just as the Welsh completed their work, almost a century later, it was taken from them, in 1283, by the English army under King Edward I. Here is thought to be the birth-place of Llywelyn ap Gruffydd, the Welsh Prince of Wales whose head was carried in London in 1282 and exhibited on a spear with a wreath of ivy.

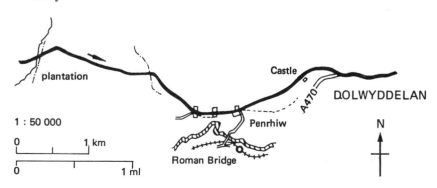

For much of the thirteenth century this was a royal residence of Welsh Princes. From the top of the keep one may enjoy a panorama of the enchanting Lledr Valley and of all the surrounding peaks where scouts would have been in clear view of this excellently-sited command headquarters.

From the north side of the Castle follow the farm track E/SE to the A470 (19.2km), turn left and continue to Dolwyddelan PO (20km, 12¹/₂ml).

Dolwyddelan – Pen-y-Pass: 15.8km, 9.9ml

Like mountain walkers of today, the ancient Celts did not keep to one route. Between Dolwyddelan and the Nantgwynant Valley they used at least two trackways, one to the north of the Afon Lledr, the other to the south.

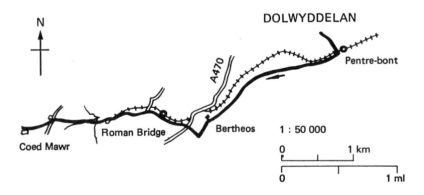

From Dolwyddelan PO (00km), bear SE over Pont y Llan and the railway bridge, fork right and right again (0.4km) along a farm drive (W). After passing a gate, fork left past the farmhouse Llwyn (0.8km), and continue W and SW along a grass path with a view of the Castle across the valley and the mass of Moelsiabod behind.

About 40m beyond the yard gate at Bertheos (2.3km), fork right (SW) from the cart-track and continue across a stream to a stile (2.8km). Turn right (NW) along the farm road, cross the A470 (3.1km) and continue westward along a council road past Pont Rufeinig (Roman Bridge) railway station (3.5km) to a farm drive (3.8km) which leads to the farmhouse Gorddinan (4.0km).

Fork right and continue to a bridge spanning the railway (4.4km). Veer left (W) and follow the path down the field to a footbridge (4.6km) and on to another footbridge (4.8km) which spans the infant Lledr. Continue W, passing a quarry pool (5.1km) on the right, across a council road (5.3km) and along a farm road to Coed Mawr (5.8km).

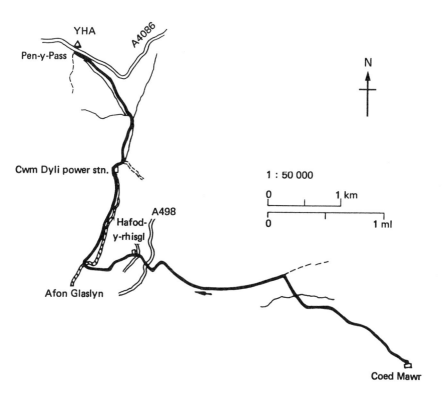

The route of the ancient trackway bears 290° up the hill, moving round the mass of Siabod with a view of Snowdon's peak ahead, to a footbridge over the Afon Cwm Edno (7.9km) and on to a junction with the east–west trackway (8.3km). Turn left (W) and continue to a ridge (9.9km) beyond which is a view of Llyn Gwynant. Continue downhill through a belt of woodland and across the A498 (10.8km) to Hafod-y-rhisgl (11.2km). This site was once owned by the Abbey of Aberconwy and later by the Wynns of Gwydir. The present house dates from the early seventeenth century. Later, it is said to have been used as a meeting place by religious dissenters.

Continue SW across a stream (11.5km), veer left along a stream path then W across the valley floor to footbridges (12.0km). Turn northward and follow the track upstream to the Cwm Dyli power station (13.6km). Cross the footbridge and turn left from the road (13.8km), ford the Afon Cynnyd and continue northward. Ford the Afon Trawsnant (14.5km) and veer to north-westward up to Pen-y-Pass (15.8km, 9.9ml) .

Here at the head of the Pass an ancient trackway, a Roman road and a packhorse trail lie beneath the modern road that descends to Llanberis and Caernarfon.

Returning to Capel Curig we may walk a trackway/trail to the southern periphery of Eryri.

Capel Curig –Ysbyty Ifan: 22km, 13.8ml

Capel Curig – Pont Cyfyng – Dolwyddelan: 8.2km, 5.1ml.

From the Capel Curig PO (00km) bear SE to Pont Cyfyng (2.0km) and turn right over the bridge which spans the Afon Llugwy as it plunges in full spate from the falls.

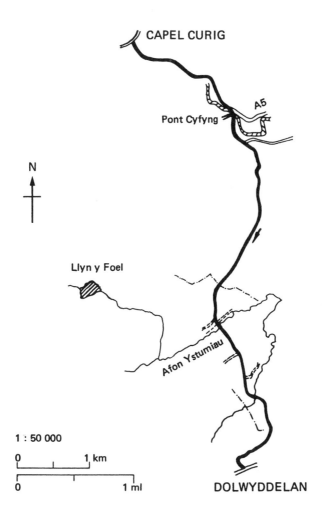

Continue through the hamlet to a turning right (2.6km) and on past a chapel (140°) on the left. Follow the track up to the ridge (3.6km 2¹/₄ml) and stand facing the mountain as the packhorse drivers must have done after pulling up from the valley. Here on Siabod's big toe, Snowdonia's weathercock seems to have shrunk to a symmetrical hillock. On a farther toe (NW) the quarrymen's quarters stare hollow-eyed down the beautiful Llugwy Valley; and everywhere about is empty and silent save for the bird calls and a breeze blowing down from the peak.

Southwards, there is a gate at the plantation boundary (4.9km) where the track disappears under a forest road. At 5.5km, and again at 6.8km, one crosses the *Afon Ystumiau:* meandering river. It rises from *Llyn y Foel* – lake of the bald top (Siabod) – and drains the moorland before emptying into the Afon Lledr.

At 7.3km veer right (210°) along the old trail, fork right 100m further on, through a gated opening (230°) and continue along a field path to a critch-cratch (7.8km) and on to Dolwyddelan PO (8.3km, 5.1ml).

Dolwyddelan – Penmachno: 7.3km, 4.6ml.

From the PO (8.2km, 4.6ml) bear SE to Pont y Llan, fork left after crossing the railway bridge and continue to the end of the village lane (8.8km).

The old packhorse trail, one of the best examples in Snowdonia, follows the course of the Afon Bwlch-y-groes upstream. But the hillside is now extensively scarred by a new forest road which effectively obliterates the trail from 9.1km to 10.3km where there is a field gate. Continue uphill (SE) from the gate, through a wall opening (10.6km) to a stile (11.1km, 7ml) in Bwlch-y-groes where the high mound on the left (elevation 455m, 1480ft) bears north. *Groes* refers to a cross or crossing; *bwlch* is a gap. *Bwlch-y-groes:* gap in the crossing.

Here is a patch of flat ground which provided a traditional meeting place for people from Dolwyddelan and Penmachno. At least until the end of the eighteenth century, villagers met here to compete in sporting activities. These were gatherings for men only, as the competitions were strictly tests for male prowess. There were tugs-of-war, wrestling matches and javelin throwing; and the location was sufficiently secluded to indulge in cock-fighting.

OLWYDDELAN

N

Bwlch-y-groes

Pigyn Esgob

PENMACHNO

1 : 50 000

0   1 km

0   1 ml

From the stile (11.1km, 7ml) the trail bears 160°, veering to 140°, rising to the ridge after 300m (11.4km; elevation 427m, 1450ft) where the next landmark stands out clearly. It is a rock scone mounted on a dome and known as Pigyn Esgob (110°). But the early travellers who named it saw it differently. *Pigyn* means thorn, *Esgob* Bishop. *Pigyn Esgob:* Bishop's Thorn.

Down from the ridge to a wall gate (12.0km), along the wall on the right to a wall opening (12.2km), around the base of the Thorn (12.3km), turn S (12.5km) and follow the stream path to a gap in the plantation (12.8km). Turn left (070°) and follow the path down to a council road (13.4km).

Listening to the gurgling sound of a stream in full spate reminds one how those early travellers used the course of streams as navigation guides. We climbed from Dolwyddelan along the course of a stream. Now, the stream one hears beside the trail, which has become a road, is finding its way to the next valley. We follow it S, then E, to Penmachno (15.5km, 9.7ml).

Penmachno

Emerging from the forest one can imagine the village as it would have appeared to a packhorse driver: a settlement built of rocks from its surrounding hills. It inherits all the historical periods since the Ice Age: Stone Age peoples have left evidence of their flint workings in the Glasgwm Valley, south-west of the village; Bronze Age people in the building of cairns over their graves, a practice that continued into early Christian times. In the churchyard and nearby are five early Christian tombstones, one of which records a person as lying "in hoc congeries lapidum" – in this heap of stones. Another mentions the mid-sixth century Consul Justinus; and another, of the fifth or sixth century, refers to Vendotia, the Latin name for Gwynedd.

Penmachno describes the *head* of the Machno, although the river's head waters are some four miles upstream, trickling across Sarn Helen, the track between the Roman forts, Tomen-y-mur and Caer Llugwy, from where it flows down through Cwm Penmachno, nestling against its derelict slate quarries.

At the centre of Penmachno is Pont Llan, spanning the Afon Machno with five flattened elliptical arches. The bridge was re-built in 1785 for £200. In the locality are several sixteenth and seventeenth-century farmhouses, listed below. Solidly built with massive stone walls, huge fireplaces, oak beams and curved stone lintels, most of them still function as working farmhouses, giving an impression of what life was like for those living in this part of Wales three or four hundred years ago.

	map ref:	period:
Ty Mawr	770524	16c
Bwlch-y-maen	782531	17c
Fedw-deg	789533	16c
Coed-y-ffynnon	804530	16c
Bennar	794518	16c

Hafod-dwyryd, with barn and outbuilding	790499	17c
Pen-y-bryn, with barn	787503	17c
Blaen-y-glasgwm (uchaf/isaf)	766495	16c
Pen-y-bedw (uchaf/isaf)	780484	17c
Dugoed	806522	16c
Dulasau-isaf	822526	16c

Penmachno – Ysbyty Ifan: 6.5km, 4.1ml.

The village road bears 200° from the Machno Inn (15.5km) for a distance of 100m, where it turns to 100°. Face a steady climb up the hill, with a sound of flowing water just off the track reminding one again how old-time travellers made use of stream courses to find their way. At 17.0km fork left (SE) passing Llanerchigwynion (17.2km). Here is one of

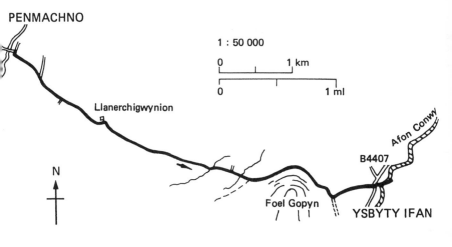

those long Welsh names which beg to be interpreted. *Llanerchi* refers to open spaces; *gwynion* means white. *Llanerchigwynion:* white open spaces. The aptness of the name can be appreciated now we are left with an unimproved track as it must have been when last used as a packhorse trail.

Plodding up to the ridge (18.1km), one is conscious of there being a point where a traveller leaves one valley and enters the next. From the top of a stile 100m further on there is no glimpse of Ysbyty, only a sense of real solitude in an expanse of open space. In places the trail is about six feet below field level: how many centuries has it taken to tramp the earth so deep?

At the bridge known as Pont Blaen-Eidda (19.6km) there is a feeling that habitation is near but still the mound of Foel Gopyn has to be by-passed. Beyond the entrance to Foel Gopyn (20.8km), Ysbyty suddenly comes into view (21.1km). Turn left (070°) and follow the track down, joining a farm road (21.6km) which leads to the village (22km, 13.8ml).

Ysbyty Ifan

Standing near the junction of the village road with the B4407 (map ref: 84174883) one can visualize Ysbyty Ifan as it was before the Second World War. Here is a mill with its wheel still in place, a pair of cottages, a wheelwright's joinery shop, a smithy – all silent now but providing a vision of the days when the village was alive with work and purpose; when farms needed men and horses, and people found most of their supplies locally. Those who worked away from the village – in the slate quarries of Ffestiniog, for example – would start their weekends by tramping across the mountains to their homes; for this was a place that people came back to; a village of singers, chapel societies – and especially legendary hospitality, a tradition that can be traced back to Ysbyty Ifan's founding.

According to Archdeacon Thomas who wrote a history of the diocese, an extract from which is displayed in the church, a hospital (or hospice) was established here, about the year 1190, by Ifan ap Rhys. *Ysbyty* means hospital. The hospital stood to the west of the present church on ground which once served as a village green but is now built over. Ifan obtained for his hospital the privilege of a sanctuary which meant that travellers could find here safety from pursuit – even from authority. It was a refuge and resting place for any traveller in these wild mountains. During the time of Llywelyn the Great the sanctuary was apparently extended to take in most of the valley including the area of Llyn Conwy. The hospitallers were called knights rather than monks but they were responsible for performing divine services and administering sacraments.

Not surprisingly the sanctuary was increasingly abused as the religious fervour which supported its foundation waned. During the fifteenth century it became a shelter for bandits who plundered the area with impunity until they were eliminated by Meredith ap Ieuan, founder of the house of Gwydir.

The privilege of the sanctuary was withdrawn in Tudor times, after the dissolution of the monastries. But Ysbyty Ifan's reputation is monumental. The bard, Dafydd Nanmor, described hospitality thus: "ei groeso fel croeso Ysbyty Ifan": his welcome was the welcome of Ysbyty Ifan.

Also unchanged is the landscape: peat moorland and rocky summits, extending out to an over-arching sky, endless
. . .

Bibliography

Jenkins, D. E., *Beddgelert: its Facts, Fairies and Folklore,* Porthmadoc, 1899.

Bradley, A. G., *Owen Glyndwr and the last Struggle for Welsh Independence,* Putnam, London, 1902.

Heywood, A., *Trefriw Guide Book,* 1905.

Jones, A., *A History of Gruffydd ap Cynan,* University of Manchester Press, 1910.

Elias, T., *History and Association of the Abbeys and Convents of the Vale of Conwy and District,* 1912.

Williams, W., *Ancient and Historic Llanrwst,* 1930.

Lloyd, J. E., *Owen Glyndower,* Oxford 1931.

Lloyd, I., *Ychydig o Hanes Foulk Roberts,* 1942.

H.M.S.O., *An Inventory of the Ancient Monuments in Caernarvonshire, Volume I, 1956; Volume II, 1960; Merionethshire, Volume VI.*

Owen, Bob., *Plas Tan y Bwlch,* Merioneth Historical and Record Society, Volume III, 1957–60; *Croesor Valley and Village.*

Nash-Williams, V. E., Jarrett, M. G., *The Roman Frontier in Wales,* University of Wales Press, Cardiff 1969.

Winson, J., *The Little Wonder,* Ffestiniog Railway Company and Michael Joseph, 1975.

Davies, G. G., *Gwilym Cowlyd 1828–1904,* Llyfrfa'r M. C. Caernarfon 1976.

Evans, D., *Bywyd Bob Owen,* Gwasg Gwynedd, 1977.

Roberts, M., *Oes o fyw ar y Mynydd,* Gwasg Gwynedd 1979.

Caernarvonshire Historical Society Transactions.

Ordnance Survey publications.

Acknowledgements

Simon De Koster's drawing of a packhorse trail in Wales
and
John Evans' map of Six Counties of North Wales (1–6–1795)
are reproduced
by permission of the National Library of Wales.

Appreciation is due to
the National Portrait Gallery, London
Witt Library of the Courtauld Institute, University of London
for material on Simon De Koster.

And to
the library service of Gwynedd County Council
and
all oral historians whose recollections have provided
unique insights about some of the thirty-one towns, villages
and locations which lie on Eryri's ancient trackways, Roman
roads, packhorse trails.

And especially to
Mrs Jane Evans (Nain), Llanrwst
Tudor Jones, on Rachub
Harry Owens, on Beddgelert and Pont Cyfyng.

And to Alwena, for reading, research, evaluation.